Training Practice

Penny Hackett is Executive Director of the Learning and Skills Council Wiltshire and Swindon. Formerly Chief Executive of Eastleigh College of Further Education, she has many years' experience as a training practitioner and lecturer. She has written a number of books for the CIPD and is currently a member of the Membership and Education Committee.

The Chartered Institute of Personnel and Development is the leading publisher of books and reports for personnel and training professionals, students, and for all those concerned with the effective management and development of people at work. For details of all titles, please contact the Publishing Department:

tel: 020 8612 6200
fax: 020 8612 6201
e-mail: publish@cipd.co.uk
The catalogue of all CIPD titles can be viewed on the CIPD website:
www.cipd.co.uk/bookstore

Training Practice

Penny Hackett

Chartered Institute of Personnel and Development

Published by the Chartered Institute of Personnel and Development,
151 The Broadway, Wimbledon, London SW19 1JQ

First published 2003
Reprinted 2004 (twice), 2006 (twice), 2007, 2008 (twice)

Design by Fakenham Photosetting, Fakenham, Norfolk
Typeset by Intype Libra Ltd
Printed in Great Britain by The Cromwell Press, Trowbridge, Wiltshire

British Library Cataloguing in Publication Data
A catalogue of this manual is available from the British Library

ISBN 0 85292 980 3
ISBN-13 978 0 85292 980 3

The views expressed in this manual are the author's own and may not necessarily reflect those of the CIPD.

The CIPD has made every effort to trace and acknowledge copyright holders. If any source has been overlooked, CIPD Enterprises would be pleased to redress this for future editions.

Chartered Institute of Personnel and Development
151 The Broadway, Wimbledon, London SW19 1JQ
Tel: 020 8612 6200
E-mail: cipd@cipd.co.uk   Website: www.cipd.co.uk
Incorporated by Royal Charter.   Registered Charity No. 1079797

Contents

List of Tables

List of Figures

Training in organisations

CHAPTER 1

CHAPTER OBJECTIVES

When you have read this chapter you should be able to:

- define training and explain how it is different from learning

- explain why training is important

- identify the main roles and responsibilities in training

- list at least four factors which influence the effectiveness of training

- explain at least three ways in which current UK legislation affects the trainer.

WHAT IS TRAINING?

Most of us have, at some time, been a 'trainer'. As the dictionary definition of training confirms, people, animals, even plants, can be 'brought to a desired standard of efficiency, condition or *behaviour* by instruction and practice'. Whether you have helped a colleague to master a particular work routine or a puppy to conform to acceptable standards of domestic behaviour, if you have been involved in changing behaviour, you have been a trainer.

Training can be divided into a number of different elements. Each may be carried out at several levels, in different ways and at different stages in the employment relationship. These elements are:

- identifying training needs – in the light of the overall objectives of the organisation and the specific requirements of individuals
- planning and organising training to meet those needs
- designing and delivering it
- evaluating the effectiveness of training.

Work to these four ends lies at the core of the training *function* – whether that is carried out by one person or several, inside or outside the organisation. By approaching each step systematically, the process of *learning* can be made more efficient.

Before we explore these elements in any more detail, there are three sets of terminology which require explanation to avoid later confusion.

Training and development

Both training and development are about changing behaviour. The terms tend to be used in different ways by those who specialise in the field. There are several different bases for the distinctions they draw.

- Sometimes the distinction is based on the *end* towards which each is directed. 'Training' is usually used to describe activities which are intended to help the person being trained (the *learner*) to conform to a particular pattern of behaviour or to reach a set standard. It implies an expectation that there is a correct way of operating and a desirable level of performance which can be directly measured. 'Development' on the other hand, is often seen as something which is on-going, with no finite end point.

- As Malcolm Martin and Tricia Jackson suggest in their book *Personnel Practice*, another distinction relates to the *content* of what is to be learnt. While 'training' may be appropriate for the acquisition of manual and technical skills, 'softer' skills like leadership and teamworking require continuous development. For this reason, some organisations still separate management development from operator training.

- The third distinction lies in the emphasis each implies on the needs of the organisation versus the needs of the individual. 'Training' can be seen as very much about getting the job done. 'Training the workers' may sit alongside 'maintenance of equipment' or 'provision of raw materials', as just one of the factors needed to produce the required output. 'Development' on the other hand, tends to focus much more on the persons themselves, and on helping them to grow in the longer term.

These sorts of distinctions are not particularly helpful today. The flatter structures which are now a feature of many organisations have tended to reduce the number of rungs on most career ladders while broadening the skills required at each level. This increase in the complexity of many roles has been accompanied by a change in management philosophy which we will discuss shortly. Many more people now need the chance to develop and grow which was once reserved for the high-flyers.

Education and training

If the distinction between training and development is less clear than once it was, the same can also be said of that between education and training. While 'training' used to be seen as particular to a type of work and even to a particular employer, 'education' was thought of as more broadly based 'training for life'. If 'training' was a means of ensuring that specific tasks were carried out in accordance with a predetermined procedure, 'education' was intended to open people's minds, to enable them to work from first principles and to question pre-ordained procedures.

Changes in both education and training have led to a blurring of these distinctions. *Vocational* qualifications prepare people for work in particular fields – like business or catering. *Professional* and *occupational* qualifications equip them for particular roles – such as personnel manager or chef. The vocational 'A' level (replacing the GNVQ Advanced) and the vocational GCSE, combined with the increasing proportion of undergraduates studying for vocational degrees, and employers requiring staff with relevant specialised qualifications, mean that educational establishments do now need to relate to the demands of particular types of work. Abstract, academic, theoretical study is no longer what much of education is about.

Conversely, development of underpinning knowledge and technical understanding now form part of the originally purely practical National Vocational Qualifications (NVQs) or Scottish Vocational Qualifications (SVQs). Foundation Modern Apprenticeships and Advanced Modern Apprenticeships now blur the boundaries still further, as many are undertaken partly in the workplace and partly at a College of Further Education or through a private training provider – see *Who is involved?* later in this chapter.

The ending of such distinctions is not necessarily a bad thing – for two main reasons:

- For more than 100 years, the UK, unlike other countries, has tended to regard 'vocational' education as inferior to 'academic'. This deterred many able pupils from pursuing a vocational education. It also made many of those who might have benefited from a vocational education drop out altogether. Currently more than 20 per cent of school-leavers vote with their feet on leaving school and participate in no further formal learning. In some areas the proportion is much higher.

- From the learners' point of view, what matters is the outcome of their learning. They may measure this directly, in terms of 'the things I can do now that I couldn't do before', or indirectly in terms of 'the qualifications I have obtained'. Since both education and training can and do provide both sorts of outcomes these days, the distinction between them is irrelevant.

Training and learning

If some of the distinctions between 'training' and 'development' and 'training' and 'education' are becoming obsolete, the distinction between 'training' and 'learning' is more important than ever. 'Training' is something one person does to another. 'Learning' is something we can only do for ourselves.

'Learning' may happen informally, in an unplanned and unstructured way, as people experiment, with or without external advice, to find the best way to get the job done. It may also happen formally, in response to a conscious decision on the part of the learner or his or her manager or trainer, to try to create the conditions under which learning can occur. It is this type of formal learning which is the focus of this book.

To understand the distinctions between training and learning we will examine briefly what learning entails.

Learning

only happens when the person under instruction

- grasps, mentally or physically, the subject
- translates it into words or actions that make sense to him or her
- locates it alongside all the other things he or she knows or can do, and
- does something with the new-found knowledge to make it his or her own.

The process through which this happens is known as the *learning cycle* – see Figure 1.

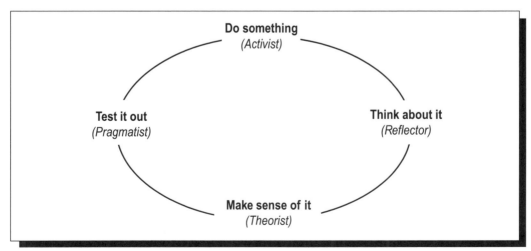

Figure 1 *The learning cycle*

Different people learn in different ways. They enter and leave the cycle at different points. But unless they work *around* the cycle to combine deed and thought (action and reflection), abstract and concrete (theory and test), their learning will not be complete.

The cycle was first identified by David Kolb in 1974, but was developed further by Peter Honey and Alan Mumford in 1986 and 1992. Peter Honey and Alan Mumford identified four main learning styles, which correspond to the four phases of the cycle. These are:

- the activist – who prefers to learn by doing
- the reflector – who likes to listen and observe, collecting data and thinking about it thoroughly before coming to any conclusion
- the theorist – who prefers to analyse how things fit into a logical framework or explanatory model
- the pragmatist – who likes to experiment with the application of new ideas to see how they work in practice, rather than endlessly analysing or reflecting.

An understanding of how the cycle works will help you

- to design individual training events and whole programmes that help everyone to move around the cycle – to embed new ways of operating into their normal pattern of behaviour. If all your training is based on presentations, however slick and well-supported by visual aids, you will never enable your audience to do much more than theorise about the subject. If they spend all their time actively engaged in practical sessions or simulations, they may never reflect sufficiently to begin to understand *why* one method works better than another. If they never grasp the underlying principles, they will be back to square one each time they are confronted with a new situation. If too much time is spent discussing the learners' own experiences, the chance to relate these to the broader theories that may explain what is happening, will be lost. Attempts to test out new ways of doing things without taking time to build on past experience and the conclusions which can be drawn from it, are likely to lead to reinventing the wheel;

- to understand, and respond to, the difficulties which some learners may encounter when they are exposed to methods that do not sit well with their preferred style(s) of learning. The action-oriented activists will need encouragement and careful coaching (see Chapter 6) to reflect on what they have been doing and to try to formulate some theories about how it could be improved – before they rush off to test them. The theorisers, on the other hand, may not respond well to role-plays and similar action-oriented methods (see Chapter 6). They may find it difficult to see what they are supposed to get from such *experiential* learning, seeing it as a waste of valuable study time. If you focus too much on discussions and other essentially participative methods, don't be surprised if some individuals are slow to contribute. They may be the reflectors whose natural style is to stand back and think about things from a number of different angles before committing themselves to a point of view. Others, the pragmatists, may tend to be intolerant of open-ended discussions. They would rather be getting on with testing out their ideas in a practical situation;

- to appreciate why, as a trainer, you may be drawn to using some training methods in preference to others. If you yourself learn best by doing, you may, without being aware of it, assume that everyone else does too. The trainer who is aware of the whole range of styles, and able to use methods appropriate to each, is more likely to be able to help a wider range of people to learn new things.

To help you assess your own and other people's preferred styles, Honey and Mumford have developed a Learning Styles Questionnaire. The accompanying booklet includes a full description of each of the learning styles.

CASE STUDY

Remotely controlled

George and Nihad have just bought themselves a new multi-channel TV and DVD player. The set is a complex one, with three separate remote control units and three instruction manuals. Both appreciate that they have a lot to learn to operate it to its full potential. While George grabs the remote controls and starts pressing buttons to see how to change channels and switch between functions, Nihad sits down to read the manuals.

Which one of them is an activist?

WHY TRAINING MATTERS

If you work in an organisation that wants to prosper and grow, training matters. Whatever direction the organisation plans to take, it is unlikely to move far towards it if it relies solely on the skills and knowledge with which it started out. New materials, new products, new systems and techniques and above all new and constantly increasing customer expectations mean that people have to learn, just to keep up. If your organisation wants to forge ahead in its particular marketplace, you and all your colleagues will need to be open to new ideas and new ways of doing things, throughout your working lives.

Training improves the capability of an organisation. It is about making sure that everyone is able to do his or her job in a way that increases the chances that the organisation will achieve its objectives. Most people *want* to do a good job. But 'doing a good job' demands:

- capable processes
- capable people
- capable performance.

To set in context the role that training plays, we will consider each of these in turn.

Capable processes

The sequences of tasks and activities through which an organisation converts 'inputs' into 'outputs' for its customers are its business processes. The inputs will include ideas, knowledge, skill, cash and physical resources. The outputs may be anything from a comfortable night's sleep – if you are in the hotel trade – to a carrier-bag full of groceries – if you are in food retailing – to an attractive and secure home – if you are in domestic house-building.

The processes are the threads running *through* the business. They are the channels along which effort, materials, information and other resources flow. If processes are well designed and functioning, they will ensure your customers' wants are met. If they are not, everyone in the organisation will spend a disproportionate amount of time disentangling them.

In a hotel, for example, the laundering of dirty linen, the provision of courtesy refreshments and the replacement of defective light-bulbs might be the responsibility of different individuals. But if the guest is to find a properly equipped room on arrival, the process through which these things are brought together must work smoothly.

If the process has not been properly designed, the person who notices a defective light-bulb first will not know who to tell or what to do about it – so it will go unremedied. Alternatively, two or even three employees may all notice the problem and turn up clutching the solution.

Your guests will not be interested in *who* deals with the problem. They would rather not be aware that a problem existed in the first place. So if gaps, bottlenecks and wasteful duplication of effort are to be avoided, the part that each employee should play and the steps that each should take must be clearly identified at the outset.

Capable people

Most people are capable of more than they, and often their employers, think they are. But self-evidently not everyone is good at the same things. People do differ, physically, mentally and psychologically. These differences are not determined by race, gender, age or disability. Instead, they probably stem from a combination of environmental and genetic factors which is not yet fully understood. In particular:

- People differ in *basic aptitudes*. Some are more likely to have the visual and spatial awareness to be able to design an aesthetically pleasing product, others may have the manual dexterity and eye for detail to build it, while others may have the innate ability with words or numbers to enable them to write good advertising copy, or price up the product.
- People differ in terms of *personality*. Some are outgoing and happy in the company of others, some prefer to work alone. Some are frustrated by rules and regulations, others need them to provide order and structure. Some relish the excitement of living dangerously, others much prefer a quieter life. Indeed, so many are the differences between individuals that psychologists spend years analysing, classifying and looking for ways of recognising them.

Training will not change a person's basic aptitudes or personality traits. It can, however, either reinforce or compensate for these inherent factors, and thereby increase people's ability to perform. Figure 2 illustrates some of the connections which will be explored in later chapters.

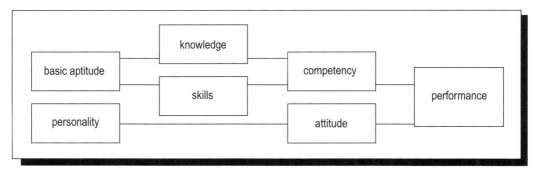

Figure 2 *Elements of performance*

Capable performance

Whether the need is for someone to sell a product more effectively, to produce it to higher quality or more quickly, or to treat customers with more care, training can make a difference. By carefully identifying any gaps between how people are doing things now and how they could be done – and then taking steps to fill those gaps – it is possible for training to have a major impact on the achievement of key results and hence the success of the organisation.

Without training

- well-designed, robust working processes will nevertheless fail to deliver the expected outcomes and financial returns. Accidents, faulty or damaged products and customer complaints are just three indicators of this
- people will fail to fulfil their full potential. If they become frustrated by this, this in turn may have one of several consequences:
  - they may leave the organisation completely and have to be replaced – at considerable expense
  - they may stay, but spend a disproportionate amount of time off sick
  - they may struggle on, under-performing in their own roles and damaging staff morale and customer relations in the process
- the performance of the team, and subsequently the whole organisation, will suffer. Some may succeed for a short time, if staff are prepared to work harder to compensate for the basic weaknesses. A few may survive on the creative brilliance of one or two key individuals or (in the public sector) be propped up by public money. But, for any organisation, enduring success is unlikely without the sustained, co-ordinated, focused effort of the whole team. This is what effective training can help to generate.

WHAT MAKES TRAINING WORK?

Training makes its best contribution to the development of the individual – and through them to the organisations for which they work – when well-motivated learners are learning something which is of value to them *and* to their organisations. To help make sense of this, further analysis of the nature of both organisations and learners is needed.

Organisations

The word 'organisation' is used throughout this book because there are few other words which embrace the range of public services, private companies and voluntary and charitable bodies which make up the modern economic and employment scene. All of them employ and/or use the skills of people – and hence may have an interest in training. Each has different reasons for being – from the provision of services like health, local government or education within a publicly-funded budget, to profit maximisation for shareholders through the design, manufacture, sourcing, distribution or delivery of all types of goods and services, to the performance of charitable acts on a break-even basis.

Ownership – whether public, private or voluntary – and the nature of their activity – production or services – are just two of the ways in which organisations differ from each other. Among the others are:

- size, rate of growth/decline
- technologies employed
- pace of change
- leadership style
- organisational climate and values
- personnel policies and practices.

We will look briefly at each.

Size

The size of an organisation can be measured in a number of ways, including financial turnover, profit, number of customers, number of employees. Clearly, it feels and is very different working for an organisation which employs a handful of people from one which employs thousands. Scale is unlikely to be the only difference. With size often comes complexity, as the organisation is structured to offer a wider range of goods or services, deal with a larger number of customers or clients, in a larger number of locations. Some very big organisations manage to keep carefully focused on what is known as their *core* business. They refuse to diversify from running buses to running railways, for example. Others see their *core competence* as operating transport networks and are happy to expand their business accordingly. Whatever the size, a shrinking organisation feels quite different from one that is growing.

Technologies

Very few organisations these days function without some degree of Information and Communications Technology (ICT). The phone – mobile or land-line, the PC, e-mail and the Internet are, to varying degrees, essential to most organisations. The complexity of the intranets required by large, global businesses will be greater than those for smaller ones, but the core technologies may well be similar. But technology is not just about ICT. The plant, equipment and systems required to manufacture machine tools or extract oil from the North Sea, or to provide same-day dry cleaning or next-day postal delivery are all very different – and so too are the range and complexity of the human skills required to operate them.

Pace of change

Very few organisations operate in static markets with a fixed customer base. Even a long-established hotel with a faithful customer base who return year after year may nevertheless find some of its clients seduced by the trendy Internet advertising of a competitor or the bargain air fares that will take them further away. At the other extreme, some ICT products have been superseded even before the customer has taken delivery. 'Change is the only constant' is a phrase used in some businesses. The environment in which organisations operate drives that change. It derives from six main sources listed in Table 1 below.

Table 1   *The PESTLE framework for understanding sources of change*

*P*olitical	Changes brought about by national or EU government
*E*conomic	Changes in the rate of inflation, interest, unemployment or other aspects of economic prosperity
*S*ocial	Changes in the birth or death rate or the characteristics of the population (demographics), such as age or ethnicity profile, life-styles
*T*echnological	Advances in medical science, ICT capability, energy production
*L*egal	Changes in statute law (new Acts of Parliament in the UK or Europe) or in its interpretation in the courts
*E*nvironmental	Public concern for 'green' issues, climate change, pollution

Leadership style

Over the last 50 years or so, many experts have tried to classify styles of management and or leadership – and to define the difference between them. One of the earliest was Douglas McGregor, who envisaged just two types of manager – *Theory 'X'* and *Theory 'Y'*. The Theory 'X' manager thinks that work does not come naturally to people so they must be bribed or cajoled into contributing. The Theory 'Y' manager thinks that all employees have a contribution to make and will make it, provided the manager gives them the opportunity. Others examined the picture in terms of the manager's concern for people relative to his or her concern for production. Blake and Mouton in their book *The Managerial Grid* (1964) developed a system to enable managers to assess their own position on a grid designed to measure these two dimensions. Today, the word 'management' tends to be used to describe the planning, organising and controlling aspects of what managers do. 'Leadership' is the part that takes the organisation or the team forward. Styles of leadership are seen as being far more varied than McGregor's or Blake and Mouton's simple two-way split. Table 2 lists six different styles currently being used by the international consultancy firm Hay Group, to distinguish between leaders.

Table 2 *Hay Group leadership styles*

Style	Primary objective
Coercive	To provide long-term vision and direction and help employees understand this
Authoritative	To obtain immediate compliance from employees by giving explicit directives and monitoring performance closely
Democratic	To build commitment and generate new ideas by inviting employees to contribute and make consensual decisions
Pace-setter	To accomplish tasks to a high standard through leading by example
Affiliative	To create harmony and promote friendly interaction and a happy workforce
Coaching	To foster the long-term professional development of employees

Managers' preferred styles are assessed using questionnaires completed by those who report directly to the manager. Those who are able to flex between several styles according to the situation are likely to be more effective than those who stick rigidly to one style – particularly if that is coercive or pace-setting. Senior managers who have a clear authoritative vision, build commitment democratically and pay attention to the long-term development of their people through coaching, are likely to provide effective leadership for high-performing organisations.

Organisational climate and values

Organisational climate has to do with the way it feels to work in the organisation and is heavily influenced by the style of those who lead it. Values are deeply-held beliefs about how to operate. Again, the history of thinking on organisation climate tends to over-simplify. One of the earliest analyses, that carried out in the middle of the last century by Burns and Stalker, distinguishes between *mechanistic* and *organic* organisations.

The first corresponds to the popular image of a bureaucracy, where there are set procedures and channels of communication for everything. Each employee has a clearly identified and restricted area of authority. Career paths are well mapped out, with promotion tending to be on the basis of length of service rather than merit.

The second is far less structured and hierarchical. Decisions are likely to be made lower down the organisation and jobs are likely to be more amorphous, adapting more readily to meet the changing needs of the organisation. The chain of command and channels of communication are more fluid. People come together as project teams and task forces to solve particular problems, without concerning themselves about the relative status of those involved.

In practice, most organisations lie somewhere in between these two extremes, and different parts of the same organisation may be at different points on the continuum. The simple dichotomy Burns and Stalker identified is no longer adequate. The Hay Group now analyse climate on six main dimensions, each of which can be further subdivided. These, together with a brief description, are shown in Table 3.

Table 3   *Hay Group dimensions of organisational climate*

Dimension	Description
Flexibility	The extent to which there are unnecessary rules, procedures, policies and practices
Responsibility	The extent to which employees are given authority to accomplish tasks without constantly checking for approval
Standards	The extent to which challenging yet attainable goals are set for the organisation as a whole and for its employees
Rewards	The extent to which employees are recognised and rewarded for good performance
Clarity	The extent to which people within the organisation know what is expected of them
Team commitment	The extent to which people are proud to belong to the organisation

As with the leadership styles, climate is measured by asking employees to rate how things are (and how they would like them to be) in relation to specific behaviours associated with each of the dimensions.

Personnel policies and practices

Some aspects of personnel policy are determined by law – see *The legal framework* below. But the leadership style and the values, which shape organisation climate, also shape the organisation's approach to setting and implementing a framework of terms and conditions of employment. Personnel policies will cover a whole raft of issues which you will find discussed in Malcolm Martin and Tricia Jackson's book *Personnel Practice*. The most pertinent ones for us to consider here are:

- performance management
- training and development.

We will start with a definition of what 'policy' is. A policy is a framework for decision-making. It is usually established by top management – the board of directors or equivalent – to guide the decisions of other, more junior managers and employees. Table 4 highlights some of the main options when developing policies.

Performance management is the phrase used to describe the alignment of employees' objectives with those of the organisation as a whole. It is about making sure that all 'rewards' whether in pay, bonuses, additional benefits, simple thankyou or more elaborate celebrations of success, are used to reinforce work towards doing the right things (effectiveness) as well as doing things right (efficiency). For example, if the objective of a travel firm is to make a profit, a reward policy which links employees' pay to the cost of sales as well as to income generated, is designed to manage their performance to achieve organisational objectives. Commission payments which reward people just for the sales income they generate, without regard to the cost of those sales, are not. To give another example, if a call centre has an objective to provide excellent customer service, performance will have to be managed to ensure that staff focus on this and not just on the number of calls handled or the average time per call. Performance appraisal – see the first section of Chapter 2 – is one powerful means of reinforcing effective behaviour.

Table 4 *Policy options*

Either	Or
based on careful analysis of organisational needs, best practice and relevant law	intuitive
formally written down as a basis for future decisions	inferred from the pattern of decisions previously made
communicated to all employees to guide decision-making	referred to after the event to justify specific decisions
prescriptive and all-embracing to minimise discretion	allowing considerable discretion
supported by operating procedures	unsupported
part of an internally consistent framework – eg recruitment and selection policies which link with each other as well as with the remuneration and reward policy and the training and development policy	stand-alone

An understanding of the organisation's policy on performance management is important to the trainer because training must be designed to reinforce effective behaviour. In some instances, employees will need to learn how to deliver quality, quantity and cost-savings simultaneously. In others, the focus will be on just one or two of these. One reason why training activities sometimes do not deliver the benefits expected of them is a failure correctly to identify just what 'performance' is required. Once this is clear, the particular behaviours that will contribute positively can be identified and trained in.

Training policy is likely to cover – explicitly or implicitly – most of the following points:

- the organisation's underlying philosophy/beliefs about the value of training
- who is eligible for training – new recruits, those recently or about to be promoted or transferred, those facing redundancy, members of designated training schemes, managers, supervisors, all employees. (Whichever categories are included, watch out for any direct or indirect discrimination on grounds of race, sex or disability. As we shall see in *The legal framework*, this is illegal.)
- what the process is for identifying training needs – see Chapter 2
- what types of training are available and on what basis – job-related only, career-related, organisa- tion-related or general; paid for wholly by the employer, or partly or wholly at the employees' expense; conducted wholly or partly in working time or the employees' own time; supported by the purchase of relevant books, software, hardware and other relevant materials or unsupported; with or without time off for revision, exams, summer schools or field work
- who will decide whether a specific training proposal is covered – and to what extent
- what the balance should be between on- and off-the-job training and between the use of internal and external resources, and on what basis such decisions should be made – cost, cost-effective- ness, urgency
- what forms of learning/learning outcomes are favoured – self-study or IT-assisted learning or short courses or courses leading to academic, vocational or professional qualifications, or distance learning

■ whether employees can appeal against decisions affecting their training – and if so, to whom and on what basis.

This brief analysis of the ways in which organisations differ would not be complete without an explanation of how organisations can themselves attempt to assess their own position. This is often done as a prelude to strategic planning, to identify potential directions for development and factors which may impede this.

The technique is called *SWOT analysis*. It involves managers and staff brainstorming the internal **S**trengths and **W**eaknesses of the organisation and identifying the external **O**pportunities and **T**hreats facing them. The action that will be needed to enable strengths to be built on and weaknesses minimised, while external opportunities are seized and threats overcome, can then be assessed. Training may form a key element of that action.

Learners

We began this section with the observation that training works best when well-motivated learners are learning something which is of value to them *and* to their organisations. It should now be clear that the things which are of value to them and their organisations must be thought about in the context of the characteristics of the organisation in question. Similarly, the things which will motivate learners, and be valued by them, must be understood.

In Chapter 6, some specific barriers to learning associated with motivation, or the lack of it, will be examined. In this section, we will take a more general look at what does motivate employees and the sorts of things they may value. For most of the past 100 years, research into the things that make people work, or work harder, has been taking place. Human beings are complex and, like organisations, differ in a variety of ways. Some would still argue that there is value in the model put forward by Abraham Maslow, 60 years ago. Maslow's *Hierarchy of needs*, first formulated in 1943, seeks to explain motivation as a series of ascending urges. The most basic need is for food, water and the essentials of life. Next in the hierarchy comes the need for safety and an environment free from threat. This is followed by social needs, such as belonging to a group and acceptance by others, and then the need for self-respect and esteem. At the top of the pyramid is what Maslow refers to as 'self-actualisation' or self-fulfilment.

While an urge or need remains unsatisfied, it acts as a motivator, but once it has been satisfied, according to Maslow, it ceases to motivate and the next higher need in the pyramid comes into play. Thus when people have acquired the basic necessities of life, they cease to be prompted by the need to get more. Instead, safety needs become paramount, and so on through to the need for self-actualisation or self-fulfilment. The main problem with Maslow's approach is the value system that is inevitably built into the hierarchy. Thus a higher order need, such as self-actualisation, becomes more respectable than a lower one such as cash to acquire basic necessities. This approach also tends to assume that once a need has been satisfied it will remain so for ever. This is not necessarily so.

Expectancy theory provides a more general explanation of motivation. It derives from work carried out initially in America by Vroom in 1964 and later by Lawler. Its main tenet is that people will be motivated to increase their effort if they believe that it will lead to their obtaining some reward or goal which they see as worthwhile. Such rewards may or may not be financial and will differ for different people or for the same person at different times. It is the employee's belief about the relationship between effort, performance, and the reward which is crucial. Thus where it is not clear that working in a particular way will achieve a particular outcome that management will reward, it won't be worth putting in the effort. Turning up half an hour early (effort) will be no use if I then find myself locked out in the cold and can't get any extra work done (performance). Even if I do get something extra done, if my manager is not going to thank me for it, or pay me a bonus or let me leave early on Friday (*extrinsic reward*), my only motivation will be the *intrinsic reward* of feeling I am in control of my work or the satisfaction I get from it.

In the particular context of motivation to learn, the classification put forward by Otto and Glaser in 1970 is helpful. They focus on the particular rewards which are involved in learning – which may be either extrinsic – providing a means to an end – or intrinsic – an end in itself. These are:

- achievement motivation, for which the reward is success
- anxiety, for which the reward is the avoidance of failure
- approval motivation, for which the reward is the approval of others – whether or not this takes the form of tangible recognition
- curiosity, for which the reward is to explore the environment and be exposed to new stimuli
- acquisitiveness, for which the reward is something tangible such as money or additional benefits.

This model has clear implications for the design of training itself and for the kinds of feedback which learners need if they are to be motivated to persevere in their learning. Since, in most cases, the learner has a choice about whether or not to continue trying to learn, the effort applied to learning can be described as *discretionary*. The Hay Group research to which we have already referred, would suggest that it is the fit between the individual's ideal organisation climate and the one in which he or she is actually working, that determines discretionary effort.

If there is one common thread running through ideas on motivation it is the importance of *clarity* – clarity regarding the roles the learners are required to perform, clarity regarding what is required to perform them, clarity regarding what to expect from training and how learning will take place, and clarity about what to expect afterwards by way of recognition, reward or other action.

Because individuals and organisations vary so widely, it is not easy to set out a recipe to ensure that learning always does work to add value to the individual and the organisation. What we *can* say is that unless management at all levels, and particularly senior management,

- is clear about the objectives of the organisation and its current strengths and weaknesses
- is clear about the requirements of particular roles in relation to these objectives
- thinks consciously about how best
  - to train
  - to reward performance to achieve those objectives via systematic performance management (see below)
- encourages learners throughout the training process, letting them see that their learning is valued and providing the kind of reinforcement and feedback they need
- devotes sufficient time, expertise and financial resource to each of the four phases of training identified at the beginning of this chapter, and in particular
- is rigorous in reviewing and evaluating the effectiveness of particular training activities as part of a plan–do–review cycle of continuous improvement,

training will not achieve as much as it could.

Not all organisations approach training in the same way. They vary in

- the amount of time, money and effort devoted to it
- the way they organise the training *function* (see *Who is involved?* below)
- the relative emphasis given to different categories of employee (most put the main stress on management development and pay less attention to basic shopfloor/operating skills – despite recent changes in the law, part-time and casual, hourly-paid staff often receive less attention than their full-time, established colleagues)
- the relative emphasis given to different aspects and types of training (organisations which depend heavily on ICT or highly technical work processes are likely to devote a higher proportion of their spend to staff in these areas).

Many of the factors discussed in this section have a bearing – from the ownership, sector, size, complexity and financial position of the business to the stability of the workforce and the range and pace of change in the skills required. Perhaps more fundamental than any of these are the basic beliefs that management holds about

- the people who make up their workforce
- the nature of the contribution they can make.

A twofold case study (see opposite) illustrates the point.

These fictitious organisations differ in several ways.

- Company A has what we may call an organisation-centred philosophy.
- Company B is employee-centred.
- Company A believes in instruction. Company B believes in coaching.
- Company A believes in standardisation. Company B believes in individuality.
- Company A believes in doing no more or less than what is essential – just enough training to stop people making mistakes. Company B believes in maximising – on-going training to enable everyone, and the company, to develop and grow. In some respects, Company B could be described as a *learning organisation*. We explore this concept more fully in the first section of Chapter 11.

Neither is right or wrong. But a trainer at work in Company A is likely to experience the function rather differently from his or her counterpart in Company B.

WHO IS INVOLVED?

Internal players

Earlier in this chapter we identified the four key elements of the training *function*. None of these presupposes the existence of training *specialists*. Line managers – who have direct responsibility for a particular part of the business and direct authority over the people who work for them – should see training as their responsibility too.

In many organisations training, or some aspects of it, *is* still seen as a separate activity. Table 5 sets out some of the possible arguments for and against separating 'manager' from 'trainer'. These options are not mutually exclusive. Many organisations get the best of both worlds by training their managers to reap the advantages of the 'manager as trainer' and use their own or external full-time trainers to add those which

---

CASE STUDY

Company A and Company B

Company A works on the basis that if every employee carries out the tasks expected of him or her, to the standard that is required, the business will achieve its objectives. Its management believes that people work best when they are told exactly what to do and are closely supervised to make sure they do it.

Every new recruit, regardless of previous experience, spends time at the company training school learning how to carry out procedures relevant to his or her particular role. Trained instructors provide structured input and keep a watchful eye on progress. Trainees are discouraged from experimenting or asking too many questions. They are expected to learn enough to meet the standard and no more. There are tests and examinations at the end of the specified training period. Those who succeed are pronounced competent and take up their roles. Those who fail may be given a short period of remedial instruction if circumstances warrant it. If they fail again they are fired.

Once qualified for their role, successful recruits are unlikely to encounter the training function again unless – as occasionally happens – they are moved to another job requiring them to operate significantly different procedures. Otherwise, 'doing as you're told' and 'not rocking the boat' are the behaviours most valued by Company A.

Company B works on the basis that every employee can contribute to the success of the business in a variety of ways. Each must be able not only to do the job but also to improve it. People are selected for their ability to learn as well as for their specific job-related skills and knowledge. An individual programme of on- and off-the-job learning is worked out between each new employee and his or her manager – to complement existing skills and to broaden understanding of the business as a whole. The pace and methods used are geared to the individual. There are specific milestones during the programme and regular meetings to review progress and redirect the style or content.

Once initial training is complete, a further programme is developed – with new as with all existing employees. Even if some elements have no direct bearing on the present job, this is not necessarily a problem. Learning to learn, to think laterally, ask questions and find new and better ways of doing things – these are the behaviours most highly prized by Company B.

Which more closely resembles your organisation?

---

derive from the more specialist route. Others increasingly see the full-time trainer as an internal consultant – see Chapter 11. Their primary role is to work *with* line managers, helping them to develop the skills they need to train their own people effectively.

The most logical conclusion to be drawn from Table 5 is that training responsibilities are best shared between line managers and specialists. Whether or not that is the case in your organisation will depend on how the role of personnel/human resource (HR) specialists in general and full-time trainers in particular is viewed.

Table 5 *The manager as trainer versus the dedicated trainer*

Manager as trainer	Dedicated trainer
Advantages	
■ best placed to identify needs ■ day-to-day contact: on-going opportunities for learning ■ possibly better technical knowledge ■ training/coaching can become a normal part of work ■ full understanding of learners' roles and responsibilities means more rounded learning ■ real examples/problems provide an effective basis for learning	■ specialist knowledge of, for example, learning theory and techniques, learning resources, external providers, funding ■ co-ordinated administration: for example, groups with shared needs can learn together cost-effectively ■ better negotiating position with external providers; easier to draw together a full picture of company needs; one focal point for external liaison ■ common learning themes for company-wide programmes
Disadvantages	
■ lack of specialist training knowledge ■ pressures of day-to-day work may restrict time ■ may not be best use of manager's time ■ managers vary in competence and commitment ■ harder to ensure consistent messages across the business ■ may be hard to get enough distance physically and mentally between current problems and general principles	■ training may still have to be done away from the job – to preserve safety, customer care, employee relationships – until the trainee is competent ■ training may be divorced from reality ■ training must usually be done in pre-scheduled doses ■ trainer may have only partial knowledge ■ trainer may still need line managers' technical input ■ learning may cease when training ends ■ line management involvement still essential, to identify needs and assess effectiveness

- In some organisations, the role of the specialist may be seen purely as a *service* – undertaking routine work which is too time-consuming for line managers to do themselves. Keeping training records is an example.

- In others, the role is *advisory* – giving the benefit of specialist knowledge but without detracting from the line manager's right to make the key training decisions. Suggestions about training materials, methods or sources of funding come into this category.

- Occasionally an *audit* role, checking that managers have complied with company policy, may be appropriate. Policing the performance appraisal system is an example.

- For some aspects *executive* authority may be vested in the training manager. This may be the case where the organisation's training budget is held centrally and the training manager has authority, in accordance with agreed policy and criteria, to determine how to allocate resources (see Chapter 10).

- Where the dedicated trainer takes on the role of *internal consultant*, he or she may be viewed by line managers as a fellow professional – proactively seeking out opportunities to make learning a way of life for all employees.

Whichever label best describes the nature of the relationship with line managers, there are still internal relationships within the training function to consider. Someone must develop the overall *policy*. Someone must *plan* how best to implement it, devising appropriate processes for identifying training needs, organising learning, monitoring effectiveness, and so forth. Someone must *put* the plans *into operation*, using the defined procedures to achieve the planned objectives. And someone must carry out the *clerical* procedures needed to keep accurate information about training numbers, costs, dates and a range of other items we consider in Chapter 9.

In some cases the same 'someone' will perform at several different levels. In others, responsibility will be divided hierarchically. Then too there is scope for specialisation within the function itself. In large organisations some trainers may focus on particular business units or divisions – eg sales or production. In others, subject specialisation may occur. One person may be an expert on finance, another on employee relations, for example.

Yet a third option is a geographical split – one person for the north, one for the south, perhaps, or if employee numbers warrant, one per site. In some organisations specialisation is by employee category – management training, technical training, clerical training, and so on. Others have a combination of two or more of these approaches.

Individual task

- How would you define your own role in training?
- Are you a dedicated trainer or a 'manager as trainer'?
- Do you provide a service, act as adviser, audit the activities of others, take executive responsibility, or work as an internal consultant?
- How proactive are you in your role?

In training, as in personnel, there is no one answer. The key to an effective organisation structure will usually lie in working out what goals the function is aiming to achieve and designing a structure to fit. However roles and responsibilities within the function are to be arranged, it will not operate effectively without an understanding of the range of external organisations which may also have a role to play.

The external training scene

Private training providers, colleges and universities are among the external providers of training to be considered in Chapter 3. There are several other bodies in the world of training with which you should be familiar. The main ones are described in this section.

The Learning and Skills Council (LSC)

This is a relatively new organisation which came into being in April 2001. It has 47 local offices, each led by a voluntary council comprising local employers, providers of education and training, representatives of local education authorities and other organisations. An executive team liaises with employers and providers to match the training and education on offer to people aged 16 and over with the skills needed in the local employment market. A national office in Coventry co-ordinates the activities of the local councils and translates the requirements of the government's Department for Education and Skills into operating policy.

The LSCs do not deliver training themselves, nor do they award qualifications. Instead, they contract with colleges of further education and with private training providers and employers. They are responsible for planning and funding learning in their locality and making sure that it is of high quality and delivers value for the taxpayers' money.

Among the priorities set for them by the Secretary of State for Education and Skills is the work of tackling the lack of essential literacy, numeracy and IT skills experienced by more than 6 million adults in the UK. They are also charged with helping employers to develop their work forces more generally – see Chapter 10. The specific targets they are expected to take the lead in delivering are set out in Table 6.

Table 6   *Learning and skills targets*

> By 2010, to ensure that 90 per cent of young people by age 22 will have participated in a full-time programme fitting them for entry into higher education or skilled employment
>
> By 2004, to increase by 3 percentage points the number of 19-year-olds who achieve a qualification equivalent to NVQ2, compared to 2002, with a further increase of 3 percentage points by 2006
>
> In 2004, to increase the proportion of 19-year-olds who achieve level 3 qualifications to 55 per cent
>
> By 2007, to improve the literacy and numeracy skills of 1.5 million adults and young people
>
> By 2010, to reduce by at least 40 per cent the number of adults without a level 2 qualification, with 1 million adults currently in the workforce to attain level 2 standard between 2003 and 2006
>
> Following consultation, to set challenging targets for minimum performance and value for money in colleges of further education and other providers

Investors in People UK

Among the ways in which the LSC can recognise the extent and value of an employer's commitment to training is the award of Investors in People (IiP). This national standard provides a benchmark for organisations of all sizes to assess whether they have in place the key elements which form the basis of business development and success.

The standard is a rigorous one and requires organisations to show that:

- They are committed to developing all their people to achieve business objectives.
- They plan how the skills of individuals and teams are to be developed to achieve these goals.
- They take action to deliver effective training for new and existing employees.
- They evaluate the effectiveness of their investment in training – in terms of its effect on individuals, teams and the achievement of business results.

While many organisations do *some* of these things for all their employees, and others do all of them for *some* employees, not all are able to satisfy the assessors engaged by IiP UK that they do *all* of them for everyone. Your local LSC will be able to explain the process for gaining recognition as an Investor in People. The benefits can be significant. Many companies have found that a focus on training and development can bring about real improvements in business performance. And with some larger organisations now looking for IiP accreditation throughout their supply chain, it can have real commercial benefits too.

Sector Skills Councils

These organisations are still in the process of taking over from the network of National Training Organisations which they are replacing. The government's intention is that the councils, by drawing together employers and others with an interest in particular employment sectors, will define the standards of competence required within the sector and set up appropriate routes to achieve them, via Modern Apprenticeships (see below) and higher education.

Qualifications and Curriculum Authority (QCA)

This is the body that oversees all officially recognised and approved academic and vocational qualifications. It is responsible for ensuring consistent standards between the organisations making the awards (the Awarding Bodies) and from one year to the next. They operate within a Qualifications Framework to help individuals and employers understand how one qualification relates to another. There are four levels – level 1 representing GCSE below grade 'C', level 2 equating to two grades 'A' to 'C', level 3 corresponding to two 'A' level (now split into AS and A2), and level 4 at Higher National level. A further, overlapping framework classifies courses of higher education through from foundation degree/Higher National to post-doctorate.

The importance of formal qualifications increased significantly during the twentieth century. In the 1950s only about 5 per cent of the population was educated to degree level. Now more than 30 per cent engage in higher education, and the government target is for 50 per cent of the under-30s to have experienced higher education by 2010. Alongside this, there has been a proliferation of qualifications and part-qualifications with, at one stage, as many as 17,000 recognised qualifications.

A number of bodies, including universities, professional institutes like the Chartered Institute of Personnel and Development (CIPD) and examining boards like Edexcel, City and Guilds and OCR can and do accredit qualifications within the QCA framework. Extensive quality assurance, verification (to confirm accuracy of assessment) and moderation (to ensure consistency of standards) take place at individual provider and Awarding Body level to ensure that, for example, the Certificate in Training Practice awarded at institution A is of a standard comparable with that at institution B, and that both conform to the standard required by the Awarding Body – in this case the CIPD. In Chapter 3 we consider the advantages and disadvantages of encouraging employees to undertake externally accredited learning. But to be sure that employees are skilled to a particular standard, an accredited qualification is one way to do it. Efforts to streamline qualifications and make them more readily understandable have led to the system of National Vocational Qualifications.

National Vocational Qualifications (NVQ)

Unlike traditional academic qualifications, NVQs focus on competences – that is, the ability to do something – rather than just the underlying theoretical knowledge or skills. They are based on occupational standards set by employers to meet the needs of their particular industry and relate to the things people have to do to show they are competent in a job. In many industries and professions, traditional qualifications have now been integrated with or superseded by NVQs or Scottish Vocational Qualifications (SVQs).

NVQs are earned through on-the-job or continuous assessment rather than by traditional examination, and do not always require additional *training*. Instead, they focus on raising awareness of learning that has already taken place. The candidate may be asked to produce a portfolio of examples of recent work or give a practical demonstration. Where training *is* needed, it can be carried out either in-house or by an external provider (Chapter 3), so long as the subsequent assessment is carried out by a qualified *assessor*.

NVQs are available at five different levels:

level 1
foundation skills
    level 2
    operative or semi-skilled
        level 3
        technician, craft, skilled and supervisory
            level 4
            technical and junior managerial
                level 5
                chartered, professional and senior managerial.

Each qualification is made up of a number of *units of competence*. Each of these comprises specific elements which are assessed against relevant *performance criteria* – see the second section of Chapter 2. Careful monitoring and recording of progress is essential, as is close liaison with the LSC to make the most of any funding which may be available – see Chapter 10.

Many employers have found that encouraging employees to work towards an appropriate NVQ raises their self-esteem as well as enhancing their skills. Some have arranged for their own managers and/or training instructors to qualify as assessors so that much of the work can be done in-house. A *verifier*, appointed by the awarding body, checks periodically to make sure that standards are being maintained. NVQs are now very much part of the national training scene, and many other qualifications have been designated as 'equivalent' to a particular level. Your local college of further education should be able to work with you to identify suitable programmes for your employees.

National Training Schemes
'Time-served' apprentice schemes used to be the only means of entry to a career as a craftsman. The on-the-job training received during the four- or five-year term was sometimes variable in quality but some consistency of standards was provided by the City and Guilds or other examinations for the day, evening or block-release classes that underpinned them.

Today's Foundation or Advanced *Modern Apprentices* are more likely to be on shorter programmes of up to three years, devised to meet the needs of particular areas. The combination of on- and off-the-job learning is still a key feature, as is the attainment of an NVQ at level two or three with an appropriate technical certificate and assessment of key communication, application of number, IT and other relevant skills.

Modern Apprenticeships can provide a fruitful source of committed recruits to the organisation, and their value is likely to increase as they progress with their qualifications. The subsidies available to help with the costs of training are certainly worth discussing with your local LSC who should be able to put you in touch with a local provider who can help if your organisation is not large enough to set up its own scheme. You can find out more information at www.realworkrealpay.info

THE LEGAL FRAMEWORK

One of the most exciting things about training is the opportunity to contribute to the development of people and organisations. But neither the organisation nor the trainer can focus only on what *they* want to do. As a key player within the human resource function, the trainer has a particular responsibility to ensure that training and development opportunities are designed and delivered in accordance with the prevailing legal requirements and good professional practice.

The relationship between employers and employees is governed by 0

- the contract of employment
- employment law.

The contract of employment

The contract is a key legal reference point for both parties. The main terms should be put in writing and given to the employee within one month of starting work. Even where this has not happened, a contract will still be deemed to exist if the employee has undertaken or agreed to undertake work in exchange for payment and certain other conditions (detailed in *Personnel Practice* by Malcolm Martin and Tricia Jackson) are met.

Contracts, which are enforceable through the civil courts in the UK, define what each party may expect of the other. Their terms cannot be changed without the agreement of both parties. Any contractual entitlement, including one to receive training, to participate in performance appraisal or to take time off to take part in training associated with the work of a recognised trade union, is enforceable in law. If the employer fails to provide it, or the employee refuses to take part in it, the party reneging on the contract is said to be 'in breach'. If it feels strongly that the particular clause should be enforced, the other party can seek compensation for loss suffered as a result of the breach or declare the contract at an end.

If the employer is in serious breach, the employee may quit the job and claim that he or she has no alternative but to do so. He or she can then make a claim to an employment tribunal for *constructive dismissal.* Where the employee is in serious breach – eg by refusing without good cause to attend a residential programme where contractually he or she is required to do so – the employer would be wise to treat this in accordance with the disciplinary procedure. If proper investigation shows that the request by the employer is justified and the employee's refusal unreasonable, transfer to another role, a written warning or even dismissal may be justified.

Contracts of employment confer a number of important rights on the individual. These include the right not to be unfairly dismissed and the right to operate under specified terms and conditions of service. The employer is obliged to pay National Insurance contributions and to deduct income tax on behalf of the Inland Revenue for its employees.

It is important for the trainer to be clear who does, and who does not, qualify for a contract of employment. Consultants, temporary staff, and those supplying services such as cleaning and catering if they have been subcontracted (or *outsourced)* to another company, may operate under a contract *for* services rather than a contract *of* service. They will not therefore be entitled to the rights which a contract of service provides.

If you engage the services of an external training provider, you need to be clear that you are not incurring the responsibilities associated with a contract of employment and can dispense with his or her services, in accordance with the terms agreed, when the work is finished. Make sure that external training providers are liable for their own National Insurance, income tax and, where applicable, VAT, before engaging them or you could land your employer with some unexpected costs. To be safe, ask to see a supporting letter from the Inland Revenue or a Contractor's Certificate. This will clarify their status.

Employment law

There is a raft of Acts of Parliament and supporting regulations which comprise the legal framework for the protection of employees. Some of this is enforced through employment tribunals who can order one party to pay compensation to the other. Appeals against their decisions can be taken through the Employment Appeals Tribunal to the Court of Appeal, the House of Lords and the European Court of Justice. Other aspects, particularly those relating to health and safety at work, are dealt with through the magistrates' and crown courts which can impose criminal sanctions such as fines and imprisonment. Acts of Parliament provide the start point for the legal framework. This is augmented by the legal interpretation or *case law* that is built up as the law is tested on appeal in the higher courts.

In general the law is silent on any express duty to provide training for employees. There are some important exceptions, though.

Health and safety

The Health and Safety at Work Act 1974 (HASAWA) imposes a duty on all employers 'so far as is reasonably practicable' to ensure the health, safety and welfare at work of all their employees. The Act stipulates that this should involve attention to plant, systems of work, use, storage and movement of articles and substances, *information, instruction, training*, supervision, the working environment and the condition of the workplace and ways to and from it.

So one fundamental element of any training, from induction through to more advanced training, is health and safety. Employees must learn what to do in the event of fire or other emergency from Day 1 of their employment. They should not be expected to undertake tasks for which they have not been trained. HASAWA is supported by a 'six-pack' of regulations covering, among other things, the use of display screen equipment, manual handling and lifting. There are also regulations specific to particular industry sectors and some more general ones like the Control of Substances Hazardous to Health (COSHH) 1989 and the Reporting of Injuries, Diseases and Dangerous Occurrences Regulations (RIDDOR) 1995.

The trainer can never afford to forget that, by their very nature, novices in any activity are more vulnerable than their more experienced counterparts. Even an apparently risk-free activity, like training to train, could have undesirable consequences if, for example, a trainee not trained in manual handling is asked to lift or move training equipment and sustains injury in the process.

Outdoor training events and management development can also be high-risk in exposing trainees to the elements. The Lyme Bay canoe disaster is just one example of how what should have been a chance to acquire new skills can all too easily turn to tragedy. It is good practice to ensure that a risk assessment is undertaken before any new training activities are introduced, to see where the risks lie. Appropriate steps can then be built into the training process to prevent or control exposure to the risk.

Equal opportunities and diversity

The law assumes that employees will receive any training necessary to prevent them from harassing or victimising each other, particularly on grounds of race or ethnicity, gender, or disability, and that managers and supervisors will be trained to use disciplinary, grievance, recruitment, selection and other procedures to reduce the chances of unfair discrimination. The implications for the trainer are wider than this.

The Sex Discrimination Act 1975 first introduced the twin concepts of direct and indirect discrimination. *Direct discrimination* is where a person is treated less favourably *because* of, for example, their race or gender. Barring women from some types of training would be an example of direct discrimination. *Indirect discrimination* is where a condition is specified by an employer with which fewer members of one group can comply, if

- it is to their disadvantage that they cannot comply, and
- it can be shown that the condition is one with which fewer members of their group can comply, and
- the condition cannot be shown to be justified in relation to the demands of the job or the training course.

Refusing to recruit trainees above a particular age – if it could be shown that this disadvantaged women with children and was not relevant to the job or training – might be an example. The Race Relations and Disability Discrimination Acts extend these protections to ethnic groups and the disabled. In the case of disability, even where the discrimination may appear to be justified in that the individual would not be able to operate under current conditions, the employer will be expected to make 'reasonable adjustments' to enable a disabled person to take part.

For the trainer, the issues go far beyond who can and who cannot take part in training. The government's aim is to encourage *diversity* in employment and society, and to provide opportunities for everyone, regardless of who they are or where they come from, to realise their full potential. In designing and delivering training programmes, the trainer can play a very positive role in bringing this about.

Case studies and examples can reveal a lot about the trainer's own prejudices. If managers are always portrayed as white and male, this tends to reinforce the stereotype that only white men *can* be managers in the organisation. If the disabled never feature in case studies except as 'people with problems', you will tend to reinforce the assumption that disability is a problem for your organisation.

Encouraging diversity means more than the avoidance of direct and indirect discrimination, and embraces the differing contributions that can be made by all parts of the community. Sometimes this may mean providing additional training to support those who have arrived in the organisation without some of the skills normally expected. This could include training in written or spoken English, for those for whom it is not their first language, or literacy, numeracy and IT skills for those who did not pick them up at school. Your local LSC should be able to support you in this, financially and in other ways.

At the very least, the trainer must always be aware that inappropriate words or deeds could mean that the organisation has to defend itself in an employment tribunal if an employee believes himself or herself to have been disadvantaged, during training, by his or her race, sex or disability. The consequences of losing a case could be costly for the employer, including compensation payable to the individual and its reputation as an equal opportunities employer in ruins. Bear in mind, too, that all employees, both full-time and part-time, are entitled to equal treatment under the law.

Time off for study or training

The Right to time off for Study or Training Regulations 1999 cover one group of people for whom training is mandatory. Any employee aged 16 or 17 who has not already attained qualifications at NVQ level 2 or equivalent is entitled to 'reasonable' time off, paid at their normal hourly rate, in order to obtain such a qualification. The qualification has to be one which will enhance the individual's future employment prospects – but is not necessarily particularly relevant to the organisation in which he or she is employed. The definition of 'reasonable' is for an employment tribunal to determine (if necessary), and will depend on the circumstances of the organisation and the effect that the employee's time off has on it.

Data protection

This is the final area where the law has a major impact on training. In Chapter 10 we examine the range of information that a trainer is expected to keep about individuals and groups of trainees, as well as about training courses, external providers and other matters. The Data Protection Act 1998 applies to all personal data held in 'a relevant filing system'. Whether your training records are held on computer or in manual files, on a card system or on video or tape recordings, they fall within the scope of the Act.

This places restrictions on obtaining, recording and holding data and the uses to which such data can be put. It requires that your organisation registers with the Data Protection Registrar. As a trainer, you are not likely to be the only person who requires data that must be registered. The personnel or HR function in general, and many customer-facing departments, will also be covered, so check with someone senior about what is required in your organisation. You may well find that someone has already been identified as *data controller* for the organisation and can advise you on the implementation of the principles prescribed by the legislation. These are listed in Table 7.

Table 7   *Data protection principles*

---

1   Personal data shall be processed fairly and lawfully and in particular shall not be processed unless
   - at least one of the conditions in Schedule 2* is met, and
   - in the case of sensitive personal data, at least one of the conditions in Schedule 3* is also met.

   * Sensitive data includes anything relating to a person's racial or ethnic origin, political opinions, religious beliefs, trade union membership, physical or mental health or sexual life. Conditions cover requirements for consent and legitimate interests as well as a number of specific conditions such as the administration of justice. So long as certain conditions are met, sensitive data may be kept for ethnic monitoring purposes.

2   Personal data shall be obtained only for one or more specified and lawful purposes, and shall not be further processed in any manner incompatible with that purpose or purposes.

3   Personal data shall be adequate, relevant and not excessive in relation to the purpose or purposes for which they are processed.

4   Personal data shall be accurate and, where necessary, kept up to date.

5   Personal data processed for any purpose or purposes shall not be kept for longer than is necessary for that purpose or those purposes.

6   Personal data shall be processed in accordance with the rights of the data subjects under [the Data Protection] Act.

7   Appropriate technical and organisational measures shall be taken against unauthorised or unlawful processing of personal data and against accidental loss or destruction of, or damage to, personal data.

8   Personal data shall not be transferred to a country or territory outside the European Economic Area unless that country or territory ensures an adequate level of protection for the rights and freedoms of data subjects in relation to the processing of personal data.

'Data subjects' – the people about whom personal information is stored – have the right to inspect the data held and the right to expect that it will only be used for authorised purposes. You should not disclose information to a third party unless this has been expressly authorised.

If an employee believes that you or your organisation is in breach of the Act, he or she can complain to the Data Protection Registrar and can ask for the information to be corrected or deleted. The Registrar has a range of powers under the Act. Employers who hold data without registering it, or who use it outside the terms of their registration, can be prosecuted. Individual employees who do so 'knowingly and recklessly' can also be prosecuted. If a person suffers financial loss or physical injury as a result of incorrect data, he or she can sue for damages.

For the trainer, this is an important piece of legislation. If you record information about trainees' perform-ance, it must be accurate and capable of explanation. If you have access to personal data, such as addresses, marital status, date of birth, you must not disclose it, even to other members of your organisa-tion, unless you are sure they are authorised to receive and use it.

Over and above the requirements of the Data Protection Act, everyone involved in training must of course recognise the sensitivity of some of the information to which they have access. Although training needs are nothing to be ashamed of, some employees *are* embarrassed that they are not yet fully competent. Even if the prevailing culture is more positive, information about who needs or has had training should only ever be released on a 'need to know' basis. It must never provide fodder for canteen gossip. Files and computer records must be kept secure, to prevent any unauthorised access.

SUMMARY

In this first chapter we have tried to 'set the scene'. In particular we have:

- defined training as 'activities designed to change behaviour'
- summarised the key elements of the training process (identifying needs, planning and organising to meet those needs, designing and delivering and evaluating effectiveness) – later chapters will explore these more fully
- distinguished between training (specific, job-related, designed to develop competence/performance to a particular standard) and development (on-going to enable people to fulfil their potential), while recognising that these distinctions are often blurred and not very helpful in practice
- highlighted the importance of the distinction between training (which we can do for others) and learning (which we each do for ourselves)
- introduced the concept of the learning cycle (act, reflect, theorise, test) and the importance of work-ing around it to ensure that learning is embedded in behaviour; we also discussed the importance of knowing where trainees naturally prefer to enter the cycle (their learning style)
- explained why training is important (as a means of improving the performance of organisations)
- identified some key features of organisations (size, technology, pace of change, leadership style, organisational climate and values, personnel policy) and of individual learners – particularly moti-vation
- introduced some of the key players inside the organisation (specialist trainers, line managers, HR specialists) and outside (the LSC, Sector Skills Councils, QCA and Awarding Bodies)
- explored government influence on training practice (NVQs, Modern Apprenticeships, IiP)
- set out the basic legal framework within which the training function must operate – adherence to the terms of the contract of employment and specific legislation relating to health and safety, equal opportunities/diversity and data protection

■ emphasised the importance of confidentiality and sensitivity in handling all the information to which the function has access.

We have *not* assumed that the trainer will always be an internal specialist, dedicated to the task of training. Line managers and external sources have a key part to play in helping people learn. Later chapters will be addressed 'to whom it may concern' – that is, whoever has responsibility for the particular aspect under discussion.

Identifying learning needs

CHAPTER OBJECTIVES

When you have read this chapter you should be able to:

- define what is meant by the term 'learning needs'
- list at least four ways of identifying learning needs and four ways of gathering relevant information
- write a learning objective
- construct an outline training plan for an individual or group.

TYPES OF LEARNING NEED

It may be stating the obvious to say that not all needs are the same. Clearly someone who needs to be better at using a spread-sheet has a different need from someone who wants to improve his or her customer care. Such differences in *content* are only the tip of the iceberg.

There have been numerous attempts over the years to classify *types* of learning. For example, Bloom's Taxonomy of Learning comprises four types of learning:

- cognitive (thinking and analysing)
- affective (feelings and attitudes)
- psychomotor (physical)
- interpersonal (relationships between people).

The simpler framework proposed by Morgan and Spoor is the one we tend to use. It concentrates on:

- knowledge
- skills
- attitudes.

More recently, the concept of *competence* or *competency* has emerged. This focuses on the behaviour which results from the exercise of particular knowledge, skills and attitudes. We will explore it more fully shortly. Others have differentiated between *levels* of learning. Pedlar, for instance, sees four successive levels:

- memory – the recall of information
- understanding – comprehension of principles/concepts
- application – to the task being learnt
- transfer – to other tasks using the same basic principles or concepts.

The issue of transfer of learning is particularly important and one to which we will return. Another way of looking at *levels* of learning is to think about the ends learning is intended to achieve. In *Identifying Training Needs,* Tom Boydell and Malcolm Leary differentiate three *levels of performance* which can each be applied to organisations, groups or individuals. The three levels of performance are:

Level 1
Implementing – bridging the gap between present and desired performance – measured against *existing standard*s
      Level 2
      Improving – to achieve continually *rising standards*
            Level 3
            Innovating – doing new and better things – to produce a *step change*

Table 8 illustrates how these may apply to each of the three audiences. We will touch on all the areas of Table 8, which is taken from *Identifying Training Needs.* For the newly-formed Sector Skills Councils and their predecessor bodies the National Training Organisations (see Chapter 1, *Who is involved?*), there is a fourth area of need – that of the whole employment sector. Identifying what these needs are, and are likely to be in the future, is a key task for these bodies, but beyond the scope of our present discussion.

Table 8 *Organisational, group and individual needs at the three levels of performance*

Level of business benefit	Area of need		
	Organisational	*Group*	*Individual*
Implementing – doing things well	Meeting current organisational objectives	Working together to meet existing targets and standards	Being competent at the level of existing requirements
Improving – doing things better	Setting higher objectives, and reaching them	Continuous improvement teams	Having and using systematic continuous improvement skills and processes
Innovating – doing new and better things	Changing objectives and strategies	Working across boundaries to create new relationships and new products and services	Being able to work differently and more creatively with a shared sense of purpose

Organisational needs

These tend to derive from several specific but inter-related sources. We will consider each in turn.

Corporate objectives

The organisation may be aiming for growth in turnover, improvement in profitability or customer satisfaction, diversification, increased market penetration, heightened brand awareness or a host of other goals. Whatever they are, they will shape the direction that the trainer must follow.

For example

One of the ABC company's key business objectives is to reduce the percentage of defective units/errors which get through to the customer – an organisational improvement goal. The operations manager called on the company trainers to:

- help communicate this to the workforce and seek ideas on how it could be achieved
- provide training for line managers to help them re-think work processes and thereby eliminate problems at source, through the use of process improvement, fail-safing and problem-solving techniques
- train operators to help them identify where and why problems start, and what they could do to put things right – using statistical process control and problem-solving
- train managers and operators in new ways of working, ranging from helping managers to develop a more 'empowering' style to helping operators to master new methods of setting up and maintaining their equipment.

Because there are so many ways in which training *can* help in the achievement of corporate objectives, it is important that senior trainers are involved at an early stage. They can then

- question which objectives are to have highest priority over, say, the next 12 months – to help assess how training activities should be sequenced or, if resources are scarce, prioritised
- look for links between objectives, to establish where training should start. In our example, the 'defective' problem was the only one which related directly to output, so it probably made sense to tackle it in isolation. Had the business needed to improve productivity and/or upgrade the perceived value of the product at the same time, a more fundamental re-think would have been needed.

If the corporate objectives do point towards a major change of emphasis involving a significant proportion of employees, the trainer must take account of this – before any attention is paid to group or individual training needs. Although most other changes at corporate level should derive from the corporate objectives, there are also some specific drivers of learning needs to watch out for:

- new products
- new technology, work processes or systems
- new legislation.

New products
If the organisation's goal is to break into new markets or maintain existing ones by developing new products or offering new or improved services, this may create the need for new skills and new methods of working. Unless the plan is to 'poach' people with the right skills from other organisations (which can be an expensive and short-lived solution), there will be a need to develop the skills internally, through training. Such change may or may not be accompanied by the third driver of corporate learning needs:

New technology, work processes or systems
The decision to introduce a new telephone system or to get everyone using Outlook Express may follow from an explicit objective to improve speed of response to customers – or may be part of normal system updating. Such changes can give rise to learning needs for people in all parts of the organisation. Training in the use of such systems, to ensure that they are being used effectively and that the benefits expected

from their introduction are realised, is essential. The same goes for any other change in the systems and processes in use across the organisation, whether or not these are driven by changes in technology. A change in the structure of the organisation, for instance, may mean that established patterns of information flow and decision-making are altered. If the change is a complex one, employees will need help to embed new and effective patterns.

New legislation

Changes in the law relating to health and safety, equality of opportunity or data protection (see Chapter 1, *The legal framework*) would not only affect the work of the trainer directly, but could also mean changes in policy, procedure and working practices across the organisation. Changes in taxation law would not just affect the accountants and the payroll team but might also have to be heeded by managers taking business decisions, and so on. Again, training will be needed if the organisation is to avoid being prosecuted for breaking the law or if the new opportunities created by the change are to be benefited from.

Maintaining core competencies

It is easy to assume that it is only *change* that gives rise to learning needs. In fact, no review of needs is complete without some analysis of the current skills profile and the ways in which it does – and will continue to – enable the business to function. If your organisation relies on expertise in the use of particular equipment, specific design or engineering skills, or experience in particular marketplaces, make sure that training to top up the supply of such skills is not overlooked.

Group needs

The needs of particular teams or departments within the organisation provide the focus for the next level of analysis of learning needs. Often these follow from the review of the organisation's needs and objectives. The introduction of a new telephone system, for instance, will have a different impact on reception or switchboard staff from the impact on more casual users. Similarly, a drive to improve quality and reduce the percentage of errors will create different imperatives in operations from those in customer service. The specific role and objectives of each team have to be understood and the way work is done now, and needs to be done in the future, analysed.

Sometimes the needs of departments do not follow directly from the expressed objectives of the organisation but derive instead from particular weaknesses in performance or the need for changes in systems or ways of working at departmental level. Depending on the extent and nature of the changes in taxation law cited above, for example, that might be a case in point. Occasionally local needs may even seem to be at odds with the corporate objectives. A drive for improved quality for a line that the organisation is planning to discontinue would be an example. Particularly in larger and more complex organisations, the trainer must be on the lookout for and question such apparent conflicts. In theory such things should not occur. In practice, it is all too common to find that internal communication leaves a lot to be desired and the left hand really doesn't know what the right is doing.

Individual needs

As we move down the levels of learning need, Table 8 on page 28 provides a clear thread to follow. The task does, however, become more complex for the trainer at each level. At the organisational level, the link with corporate objectives should be the main driver and will determine whether the goal is maintenance, improvement or innovation. At the team or departmental level, the task of the trainer may be to question how team goals fit with corporate goals. At the individual level, there are three potential drivers of learning need:

- corporate objectives
- team goals
- individual goals.

Corporate objectives
The goals of the organisation may mean that some individuals need to acquire multiple skills at the same level, or progressively higher skills to equip them for promotion.

Team goals
Departmental objectives and needs may mean that some individuals have to learn to handle new processes or to improve their contribution to existing ones.

Individual goals
Employees' agendas may differ somewhat from those of the team or the organisation as a whole. Their goals for the future may include working for a different employer or at a higher level – while the employer may not be prepared to invest in transferable skills. Their assessment of their own needs may be based on a different view of the reasons for any present under-performance. Identifying individual learning needs is therefore the primary focus of the next section.

METHODS AND SOURCES

Some line managers see all performance problems as training problems and will expect you, the trainer, to provide solutions. Others will insist that their people should 'try harder' or 'show greater commitment' when it is patently obvious that there is a basic lack of vital knowledge or skill.

The trainer's job is not to usurp managers' responsibility for helping their people to meet performance standards. It is to help managers identify which problems may have training solutions and to anticipate future learning needs. This is done in different ways and at different times depending upon the organisation and its training policy. Some training interventions will indeed be 'problem-centred' as Reid and Barrington describe them. In these instances, the trainer must select sensibly from the range of methods outlined here, in order to get to the root of the problem. Where a more general review of learning needs is required, these approaches can be built into a planned sequence. All have basically the same objective – that is:

1   to establish the knowledge, skills, attitudes or competencies which are *required* to achieve the necessary standards of performance, now and in the future. This is done through the twin processes of job and task analysis or through investigation of the competencies required for effective performance

2   to assess the extent to which the individual employee *meets* those requirements. This can be done using a number of different methods, which can be used separately or combined in performance appraisal

3   to define the size of the *gap* between 1 and 2 above.

Job analysis

In *Training Interventions* Reid and Barrington make the point that what they call 'comprehensive analysis' is not always necessary. They suggest it is likely to be worthwhile

- where a completely new set of roles is being created, perhaps in a start-up situation or on the opening of a new facility

- for jobs below managerial level. The discretionary and frequently-changing nature of more senior jobs limits the extent to which performance can be prescribed and therefore described.

In other situations, a competence-based approach, as outlined below, may be more useful. Even so, for a full analysis of learning needs, the first step is to be clear about what the employee's role entails and will entail in the future. The starting point is a clear and up-to-date *job description*, highlighting the purpose of the role and the key tasks that the job-holder is expected to carry out. There are a number of different ways of analysing a job to arrive at a job/role description if one does not already exist. (If it does, it is still advisable to check that it is up to date.)

You can

- ask the employee's manager to write a synopsis of what is expected
- ask the job-holder to write a synopsis of what is expected
- ask the job-holder to keep a *diary* for a month (or longer if the job is complex with long intervals between repetition of the same task in the job cycle) so you can analyse together how time is actually spent
- *observe* the job-holder at work, *shadowing* him or her throughout a long enough period to get a real insight into the key tasks, or *sampling* at regular intervals to be sure of obtaining a comprehensive picture
- talk to the job-holder's *colleagues,* particularly if the job forms part of a team
- talk to the job-holder's *customers*, both internal and external: these are the people who receive the outputs which the job produces – whether these take the form of information, ideas, products or services – and can help you understand the part it plays in the total process
- undertake a *content analysis* of documents produced by job-holders, to identify the main outputs required.

Whichever method is used – and there is a strong argument for combining two or more of them to get a rounded picture – the finished description has to provide an accurate reflection of the type of things the job-holder is called upon to do. From the trainer's point of view, the objective is to gather sufficient detail to make sure that no vital tasks calling for completely different knowledge, skills or competencies are omitted. So once gathered, the data must be analysed and grouped. This can be done either by type of task (handling information, handling money, handling people, handling product or materials), or by level of activity (operational, administrative, supervisory, managerial), with further subdivisions if necessary.

Key task analysis

Once the content of the job has been analysed, the next step is to analyse each key task to see what knowledge, skills and attitudes are required. Unless this is done, time may be wasted training employees in how to perform the task, without recognising where they need to start from. In the rudimentary example below (Table 9), it might never be possible to train our catering supervisor to devise an acceptable menu if we overlook the fact that he or she needs some knowledge on which to base decisions about what is and is not acceptable. Without this, we need either to remove the responsibility for menu-setting from the role – perhaps asking someone else to do it, or creating a pre-set list of menus from which the supervisor has simply to select each day – or settle for the fact that food will not be available at the required times, will be too expensive, and so on.

Table 9 *Basic task analysis – a catering supervisor*

Task	Knowledge	Skills
Devise menu	Nutritional values, food preparation times, methods and resources required, cost and budget constraints	Customer awareness
Cost menu	Food and staffing costs, company costing methods	Numeracy
Order catering supplies	Ordering procedure, forms, authorisation procedures	Literacy
Oversee food preparation	Food preparation methods; food hygiene, health and safety, staff deployment	Motivating and advising cooks

Competency analysis

Reid and Barrington distinguish two main approaches to the use of competence as a basis for the identification of learning needs:

- input approaches
- the outcomes model.

Input approaches focus on the mix of aptitudes, attitudes and personal attributes which enable managers in particular to perform effectively. In analysing them, the emphasis is on the patterns of *behaviour* that people need to bring with them to the job. Reid and Barrington use the term *competency* to describe these behaviours.

The outcomes model is the model on which NVQs are based and focuses on what high performers *achieve*. Reid and Barrington use the term *competence* to describe these outcomes. Following the NVQ model, each statement of competence requires an active verb – eg 'evaluate' – an object – eg 'changes to systems' – and a statement of the conditions in which it applies – eg 'in relation to operational finance issues'. The Chartered Institute of Personnel and Development, for example, has taken this approach in developing a set of professional standards for those involved in personnel and training. The combination of vocational and academic qualifications through which these standards can be met are highlighted in Chapter 11.

We will focus here on the behavioural or input model and define competency as 'the ability to do something'. This ability, which brings together the necessary knowledge, skills and attitudes, is translated into behaviour which can be observed and measured. The characteristics of competencies are summarised in Table 10.

In recent years, some organisations have invested time and effort in attempting to define the competencies they require of employees – as a basis for recruitment and selection, appraisal and reward – as well as to help identify training needs. Where an appropriate competency framework exists, the task of establishing learning needs is relatively simple. Such *organisational* competencies are the abilities which are valued by the organisation because they are believed to have some bearing on the overall performance of the enterprise. One leading insurance company has identified six such competencies as a basis for managing performance throughout the business. These are: thinking, innovating, communicating and influencing, goal orientation, showing leadership, and professional ability.

Table 10 *Characteristics of competencies*

Characteristic	Definition
Behaviourally anchored	Are based on examples of the desired behaviour
Observable	Can be consistently and reliably assessed by trained assessors
Forward-looking	Should reflect the kind of behaviour that will be relevant tomorrow – not yesterday
Discrete	Can be individually labelled in such a way as to describe a separate set of behaviours
User-friendly	Come with a label and the associated behaviours stated in simple, jargon-free language to encourage ownership

Table 11 contains some examples of competencies. Each has a *label*, to describe what the competency is about, a *definition*, and a series of descriptions of behaviour or *performance indicators*. Other models you may come across use *clusters* of *dimensions* to provide more detailed labels and definitions of the relevant behaviour indicators.

Table 11 *Sample competencies*

Label	Definition	Performance indicators
Commercial judgement	tendency to make soundly-based decisions affecting the medium- and long-term future of the business	■ takes account of a range of internal and external factors in making decisions ■ evaluates risks in a disciplined way ■ takes calculated risks to seize opportunities
Teamwork	tendency to work with the team to identify objectives and work towards their achievement	■ clarifies goals, roles and responsibilities ■ values the achievements of others ■ manages conflicts and concerns positively ■ carries others with him or her through a range of influencing styles ■ respects and is respected by others
Communication	tendency to share information effectively with others	■ shares appropriate information openly ■ listens and responds effectively ■ maintains consistency between words and actions ■ keeps senior management informed

The definition of appropriate performance indicators is critical to the competency-based approach. Once these have been identified, standards of performance can be defined – see Table 12. Performance indicators can be derived from a range of sources. The critical questions to ask are

- ■ 'What does good look like?'
- ■ 'What is acceptable?'
- ■ 'What is poor?'

The answer may be found through

- interviews with managers to find out what they observe effective performers do that ineffective ones don't
- interviews with colleagues or internal or external customers to find out what they observe effective performers do that ineffective ones don't
- interviews with individual employees to establish which aspects of the work they find most difficult or demanding or which they regard as most critical to success.

These interviews may simply be structured around the questions above, or use more formal, repertory grid techniques. You will find guidance on interviewing in the next section. Use of the repertory grid requires grouping and cross-checking one set of responses with another, to tease out the factors that really make a difference. It is explained in detail in *Job Analysis* by M. Pearn and K. Kandola. Table 12 provides a simple illustration of the outcome of the process.

Table 12   *Competencies and standards of performance*

Competency	Definition	Performance indicators	Performance standard
word processing	ability to use specified word-processing software to produce timely, error-free documents	word processes letters and memoranda from hand-drafted text and audio dictation	■ without errors ■ in accordance with the approved house style ■ at the rate of 12 pages of text per hour
word processing	as above	word processes reports and presentation documents using imported text and graphics	■ without errors ■ using the most appropriate layout and typeface ■ at the rate of 10 pages of text per hour
word processing	as above	prepares tabulations, graphs and charts to produce word-processed reports and presentation documents	■ without errors ■ using the most appropriate format for the data ■ at the rate of five pages · of text per hour

Performance appraisal

In order to match the performance of the individual against the standards of performance required, or to assess whether he or she has the knowledge, skills and competencies needed, appraisal is an essential tool. It is the regular (six-monthly or annual) review of performance by managers and individual employees. It usually centres on performance against agreed job objectives, specific competencies, performance standards or personal goals.

A written report, agreed by both parties and perhaps a more senior manager, is usually produced and a copy given to the trainer to action the training needs identified. Alternatively, there may be a further discussion between trainer and line manager to collate departmental needs on the basis of the reviews.

In some organisations, appraisals between colleagues and of bosses are also conducted. These are sometimes referred to as 360-degree and 180-degree appraisals, depending on whether they provide an all-round view or just a vertical one.

Performance appraisal takes many forms and can serve several purposes. These include:

- identifying barriers to effective performance – including lack of training, unclear objectives, poor interpersonal relationships or ineffective job design
- enhancing employee motivation through positive feedback
- identifying additional responsibilities or changes in working practices which will assist in achieving departmental goals and/or develop the employee
- improving communication and sharing or reinforcing the vision and values of the organisation
- as a basis for determining performance-related pay and/or promotion decisions.

There are three main approaches to performance appraisal:

- traits-oriented
- results-oriented
- competency-based.

The traits-oriented approach involves the appraisal of personal qualities such as appearance, punctuality, co-operativeness. It is little used these days because it does not shed much light on actual job performance.

The results-oriented approach requires that the outcomes (results) achieved by the job-holder form the basis of the appraisal. Sales figures, wastage rates, complaints received and costs incurred provide examples.

The competency-based approach recognises the importance of the way the person goes about doing the job – ie his or her behaviour – rather than just the results achieved. It relates back to our discussion above by focusing on what the effective performer does and the specific competencies exhibited.

If systems differ in terms of what is appraised, they also differ in terms of the objectives which they are designed to serve. Some are essentially *judgemental* in their aim, assessing past performance with a view to remedying deficiencies. They typically include some form of rating or scoring system to record how well (or badly) each person is performing. *Developmental* systems, on the other hand, are more concerned to review past performance with a view to learning how to do things differently in the future. Often renamed 'performance reviews', many find it hard entirely to escape a judgemental element – particularly where the onus is on the boss to produce the report or there is an explicit link to performance management.

The review and discussion between each individual employee and his or her manager which should form the basis of the appraisal is central to the identification of learning needs. In preparing for the meeting, both sides should

- review what has been achieved in the period since the last review
- identify anything that has gone particularly well – and consider what influenced the outcome

■ identify anything that has not gone particularly well – and consider what influenced this.

In doing this, the manager in particular may want to look back over reports and data relating to the appraisee's performance and seek the comments of other managers, to try to formulate a rounded view.

If your organisation does not have an appraisal scheme, you may wish to talk to managers about the possible benefits of introducing one. Do not contemplate it unless

■ the objectives are clear. Is it to be used just for the identification of learning needs, as an opportunity for the reasons for performance to be explored, and to inform requests for additional training? Does the organisation have other needs, such as the development of a more democratic leadership style or an improvement in internal communication which the process should serve?

■ managers and staff are, or can be encouraged to become, committed to the scheme and what it entails. This will only be achieved if four conditions are met
  – the objectives are both clear and relevant to the organisation
  – all who are to use the scheme are trained in its use
  – the scheme is seen to be used for the purposes for which it was intended
  – each appraiser is appraised – preferably before appraising others

■ the basis of the appraisal (traits, results or competencies) is clear and relevant to the objectives. As a general rule, people find it easier to relate to results- or competency-based schemes than to anything which resembles restructuring their personality traits. Even with results-based schemes it is tempting for a 'blame and excuse' culture to be fostered, particularly if there is a strong judgemental element to the scheme

■ the record of the discussion is simple to produce in a manner which provides a fair record of what was said. Unstructured narrative can score on the latter but not the former aspect, and will create problems if the reports of different appraisers are to be compared – perhaps because there appear to be common training needs in different departments. Checklists can overcome some of these problems but can still prove difficult to standardise unless extensive appraiser training is used to ensure consistent interpretation. Rating scales can create similar problems and will inevitably be seen as judgemental, while comparisons between people are best avoided: if everyone is working continuously to improve, whoever starts off as the weakest performer is likely to remain the weakest, creating the *zero sum effect*.

Tips for appraisal interviewing

■ Be clear about the objectives – this is not a disciplinary interview.
■ Prepare thoroughly – make sure you know what the employee has been responsible for – and over what period.
■ Involve other people – colleagues, customers, others who have been on the receiving end of the employee's output – and encourage the employee to do the same.
■ Put the employee at ease – and make sure he or she also understands the objectives.
■ Use the interview to raise awareness and a sense of realism – not to praise or blame.
■ Ask the employee for his or her assessment of what has been achieved.
■ Use open questions – How? How often? With what results?
■ Be ready to probe further – What were the consequences? What else did you do?
■ Don't settle for generalisations – they will make the interview superficial and lose the chance for you both to get a real insight into how the employee's behaviour affects the organisation.
■ Encourage the employee to be as specific as possible – about what has been satisfying

or frustrating, what he or she would like to do more of, what other contribution he or she could make.

- Don't interrupt or contradict the employee unless you want to make him or her defensive. If you need to put an alternative perspective, try to get at it by questioning – Did everyone see it that way? What other interpretations could there be?
- Listen carefully to what the employee says – and how. Body language such as defensive gestures or an aggressive stance may mask a basic lack of confidence.
- Summarise regularly to check that you have understood what the employee is saying – and to aid your recall when writing the report.
- Use coaching (Chapter 4) to help identify how else problems might be tackled, confidence and competence increased and objectives achieved.
- Make sure that as many suggestions for improvement as possible come from the employee rather than from you. He or she is more likely to be committed to these ideas than to yours.
- For each key area, agree what will happen to achieve it, when, who will do it, and how success will be measured.
- Make sure that actions are genuinely agreed and that the employee takes responsibility for most of them. Appraisal is about helping people to think for themselves about what needs to be done and how to do it – afterwards they should be less dependent on their manager, not more so.

If you are involved in training others in the use of the scheme, you may want to incorporate some of these tips. There should be regular evaluation of the extent to which the scheme is meeting its objectives – and a process for modifying it to enable improvement.

Development centres

As an alternative to regular appraisal, or as an adjunct to it, development centres can provide a powerful insight into the extent of the learning needs of employees. They are designed to enable participants to demonstrate a range of personal, interpersonal, managerial and technical abilities or competencies, under the eye of trained observers. A profile is compiled to reflect relative strengths and weaknesses or for comparison with a predetermined job profile. From this, an individual development programme can be constructed to help overcome the weaknesses or further reinforce the strengths.

A centre usually comprises a number of different individual or group tasks or exercises, each designed to allow delegates to demonstrate one or more of the relevant competencies. Centres are usually conducted over one or two full days or even longer – depending on the number of competencies to be assessed. Groups of between six and 12 participants – and nearly as many managers trained as observers/assessors – may be involved.

The process may appear similar to that followed in group selection or *assessment centres,* but it is important not to confuse the two. Their objectives and outcomes differ significantly. Whereas development centres are designed to help plan future learning and there is no 'pass or fail' outcome, assessment centres are geared to deciding which of a group of applicants comes closest to matching the requirements of a particular job. Those deemed unsuitable should – but not always do – get feedback to help them in future job applications.

Designing and running development centres is not a job for an amateur. If you are to get involved, you will need special training. As a trainer you may be asked to

- identify specialist consultants who can help design the process
- organise training for observers to ensure that they know what they are looking for and how they will recognise, record and evaluate particular types of behaviour
- explain the nature and purpose of the activity to line managers and/or other employees
- publicise the practice so that employees who want to be considered for further development can put themselves forward
- make the administrative arrangements:
  - booking the venue – which may need appropriate indoor and outdoor facilities (contrary to what you might expect, a development centre is not a *place*, although some larger organisations do have a fixed base, such as a company training centre, which they use)
  - scheduling the events. It may be necessary to divide participants into groups so that some can do one exercise or task while others are engaged elsewhere. Both participants and observers will need a detailed, timed programme
  - acquiring the necessary resources – anything from pads and pens to mobile phones, maps and specialist outdoor equipment may be required, depending on the kind of exercises involved
  - welcoming candidates and helping to brief them on programme details
  - acting as link/continuity person on the day, to make sure that everyone is in the right place at the right time for the right activity
- assist with assessment – helping to mark written elements of the programme or assess practical elements
- draw together observers' scores and ratings to produce an overall profile
- provide participants with feedback
- design individual training programmes to meet the needs identified
- collate the outcome to feed into the organisation's training plan.

Development centres, like appraisals, are both systematic and relatively formal ways of identifying individual needs. They also require rather a lot of time and effort to set up and administer. The next method we consider can also be quite labour-intensive.

Direct observation

It is not always necessary to set up special exercises in order to observe competency levels. Watching someone at work can be quite illuminating. Provided the observation is objective and based on specific expected actions or behaviour, it will often be all that is required as a basis for identifying learning needs.

Observation may be either *open* (the employee knows it is taking place) or *unobtrusive* (the employee does not know). If, for example, your organisation has a prescribed way of answering the telephone, you can spend some time in a busy department and listen to how many staff actually do answer in the prescribed way. Alternatively, you, or a mystery caller, could ring in from outside, posing as a customer, and see what response you get.

If open observation is to be used, try to work alongside the person or people you are observing and allow them time to get used to your being there. When you first arrive, particularly if they do not know you or mistrust your motives, some may be flustered and others may be inclined to show off. Either way, you will not see them operating normally – which is what your customers do. Bear in mind that you may need to watch for a while in order to get a reasonable sample of behaviour. That is important to enable you to distinguish between one-off lapses and real learning needs.

Seek to be objective about your assessment by working out in advance the sort of behaviour you expect to see. Unless it is essential to prevent a major disaster, it may be best to resist the temptation to keep stepping in to 'put things right'. For one thing, there may not actually be a 'right' way to do it. There may be *your* way and the employee's. If the latter achieves the ultimate objective without creating undue waste, cost, quality deficiencies or other adverse consequences, interference could be counter-productive. It will, in any case, be better to observe the process from start to finish rather than tampering with it part-way through, if you are to understand fully where the needs lie.

Once your observations are complete, it is best to take a little time to reflect on how what you have seen relates to the needs of the organisation, the team or the individual's role.

Self-assessment

This method of assessing learning needs can be either formal or informal. Formal methods invite employees to rate their competency against predetermined standards at regular intervals and ask for training or other help if they feel they would benefit. Informal methods leave it up to the employee to work out that maybe some training would be useful – and leave the onus on the individual to ask for it. The response will depend on the organisation's training policy, if there is one, the attitude of the line manager, and the state of the training budget.

To help formalise self-assessment you may need to

- design an appropriate pro forma for recording and assessing competencies
- advise employees on how to complete it
- help identify which competencies are relevant to which jobs and what the appropriate standards of performance are
- collate completed assessments and group those with similar needs
- re-design training programmes and learning packages to cross-refer to specific competencies
- produce statistics and/or reports on competency levels and learning needs
- match identified needs with possible learning opportunities.

Faults analysis

Although this sounds the most negative of the approaches described, it need not be so.

It is often possible, by looking at the *outcomes* of a particular process, to identify problems which have occurred *within* the process. The stitching which fails to pass inspection by quality control – or worse, by the customer – is a fault which may be attributable either to poor equipment set-up or poor workmanship. If the former, who set it up and what is his or her level of competence? If the latter, who did the work and what is his or hers? In either case there *may* be a learning need – or there may have been a lapse of concentration caused by other factors.

Sometimes it will be necessary to pursue the fault much further. Who designed the item? Who specified the materials? Who supplied the thread? Any (or several) of these individuals may have lacked the knowledge or the skill to enable the work process to deliver to the required standard.

In these cases the 'fault' does not lie with the operator. In so far as he or she could have identified the potential for the problem to arise and failed to do so, there may actually be a fault in some other process entirely. Perhaps the payment system encourages employees to keep up their speed at all costs – or perhaps the management style of the organisation (Chapter 1) makes employees feel it is safer to keep their heads down rather than risk trouble.

Carefully implemented, faults analysis can be used on a very wide range of processes, looking at everything from clerical errors to cancelled orders and from guarantee claims to employee turnover. It can provide a very thorough insight not just into learning needs but into how the organisation really works and how inter-dependent all its processes really are. The downsides are:

- the name – which implies blame and castigation rather than help
- the time it can take to get at the root causes of a problem buried deep in the process – tackling the symptoms is a big temptation!

GATHERING INFORMATION

Interview skills

Several of the methods reviewed in the previous section require interviewing skills. The precise approach will of course depend on whether the interview is intended only to elicit facts, as in task analysis, or to evaluate them, as in performance appraisal. The checklist below gives some general tips to help.

Tips for interviewing

- Before the interview, make sure you know what you want to achieve (the *goals* of the meeting).
- Check that you have read and understood any relevant *documents* – job descriptions, procedural manuals, notes of previous meetings.
- Choose a *location* where you will not be interrupted.
- Be relaxed but professional and interested in your *manner*. Try to avoid distracting mannerisms, like playing with your hair or jewellery or repeating the same phrase or sounds.
- Plan the *structure* of the interview to make sure that you will cover all the main points and have enough time to explore key issues.
- Always start by reminding the interviewee what the *purpose* of the meeting is and how you plan to approach it.
- Encourage the interviewee to *take a lead* in identifying what is happening/what is to be done.
- Ask *open* questions – 'What?', 'How?', 'Why?' – to encourage the interviewee to give more than one-word answers – see Chapter 6.
- Ask *closed* questions – 'When?', 'Where?', 'Who?', 'Do you?', 'Have you?' – only to elicit brief factual information
- *Probe* fully, to make sure all the issues and options emerge – 'What else?', 'Tell me more about ...', 'What then?', 'What do you put that down to?'
- Avoid *leading questions* – 'So you don't spend much time on the shopfloor, then, do you?' may lead the interviewee just to agree with your assumption rather than to challenge it.
- *Summarise* regularly – to make sure that you are getting the main points and help keep the interview on track – 'So you normally get the showroom set up first thing and then review the previous day's sales. What then?'
- Don't *patronise*. Indiscriminate Thank-yous or Well done's make it sound as though you are not really listening or are not interested in the answers.
- Work to develop your *listening* skills – see Chapter 6.
- Keep careful *notes* – if possible use a purpose-designed checklist or pro forma with which you are totally familiar.

- At the end of the interview, *thank* the interviewee for his or her time.
- Allow *time between interviews* to review and organise notes and plan the next meeting.

Taking notes

Whether you are gathering information through interview, observation or analysis of documents, clear, legible notes will help you, and anyone else who may need to conduct a similar analysis or check your findings. The art of note-taking lies in distilling what is important and recording it, without the use of redundant words, in a form which enables you quickly to identify related facts and issues. Unless you are able to speedwrite or use shorthand, you will need to develop your own style.

Some people use symbols to enable them to cut out unnecessary words. Those in common use include '&' or '+' for 'and', '+ve' and '–ve' for 'positive' and 'negative', arrows to indicate direction, < and > for 'less than' and 'more than' , three dots in an inverted triangle for 'because' and in an upright one for 'therefore', and so on. Many words also lend themselves to shortening or abbreviation. The important thing is always to make sure that the abbreviation or the omission does not lose the sense of what was originally said or observed.

Notes are most useful when they

- are brief
- link to key themes or issues – numbering or lettering to denote ideas and issues that fit together is a good idea
- contain sufficient detail to make sense some days later
- are not so detailed that you might as well have written an essay.

Some people find it helpful to adopt specific structured note-taking techniques, like Tony Buzan's 'mind-mapping' in which connected ideas are joined by lines. Others like to divide their page into columns or boxes to enable them to record ideas and contributions from different sources. Yet others use 'Post-It' notes with a separate idea on each, to enable themes to be developed by grouping similar ideas together later. (This last approach is more practical when you have a desk and some documents to analyse, not when you are trying to capture what is said in an interview. If you want to experiment with the method, and time permits, tape recording the interview may help.)

Whatever method you use, giving some conscious thought to the process will pay dividends.

ESTABLISHING OBJECTIVES

Now that you think you understand the training needs of the organisation, specific teams and individuals, you may be itching to get some training off the ground. But what exactly is it that you are going to train people to do?

The answer, you may think, is obvious. Audrey has the production of customer presentation documents as one of her key results areas. She needs to be quicker at using the relevant software. Let's send her on a course and get her needs met.

But which course? Unless you delve behind the general need you may teach her the wrong things. If you do that, you will be wasting valuable time and money. Worse, if Audrey still isn't quick enough, she will become demoralised and you will lose confidence in her. Neither bodes well for her future.

Translating competencies into learning objectives

What you now need is a clear and precise set of learning objectives to enable you to plan an appropriate course of action. Only if the objectives of the training activity are specific, are measurable, are achievable, and set out how you will know when they have been achieved, will you be able to measure later the extent to which they *have* been achieved (Chapter 8}.

An objective is a statement of what the learner will be able to do in what circumstances and to what standards, when he or she has successfully completed a learning experience.

Objectives are important for three main reasons:

- By defining what the learner is to be able to do at the end, they limit the learning task, for the learner and the trainer.
- By clarifying the type of learning that is to take place, they help to narrow down the choice of learning method – see Chapter 4.
- By setting out the standard to be reached (the terminal behaviour), they establish a measurable goal and a framework for evaluation – see Chapter 8.

In our example, your aim is to identify exactly what it is that you want Audrey to be able to do after she has been trained – to what standard and at what speed and in what circumstances. That is where the standards of performance identified as part of the competency analysis discussed earlier in this chapter come into play.

Audrey's need for improvement in her text-processing skills provides a working example. You now know that what you want her to be able to do after her training is to demonstrate enhanced competency. If you have defined the competency and performance standards associated with word processing shown in Table 12 on page 35, it will be quite easy to define the objectives of her training.

The *performance standards* and *criteria* for each level of competence define the possible goals at which Audrey must aim and which her training should equip her to achieve. This will be her learning objective. Your only task now is to find out which of the three levels of competency is appropriate for her.

Each does of course represent a rather different outcome. The number of functions Audrey will need to master and the options of which she will need to be aware will be considerably greater in the second and third cases than the first. Training designed to develop only the first level of competence is unlikely to enable her to achieve the third. Conversely, she is unlikely to be able to perform at level 3 if she is not competent at level 1, so you will need to consider a step-by-step approach to helping her to reach full competence.

To establish which level comes closest to describing the required outcome, you will need to review the sort of work Audrey is required to do to see which standards of performance she really needs to achieve. If you can involve Audrey in this process, so much the better.

In this particular example, the objective finally formulated was

> *At the end of her training Audrey will be able to word process reports and presentation documents using imported text and graphics – without errors, using the most appropriate layout and typeface, at the rate of 10 pages of text per hour.*

Audrey's needs were a relatively simple example. If Ray needs to be a 'better manager', you could be looking at a number of things – from working with others to getting the best from his team, and from competency in planning and allocating resources to effective decision-making. The learning objectives you might need to define could be many and varied.

Before you decide all this looks far too time-consuming, remember you do not have to reinvent the wheel every time you look at competencies. Although, as we saw earlier, their focus is on outcome rather than behaviour, the structure of the NVQs described in Chapter 1 is such that, for many jobs, from management to operative, and across industries, from retail to construction, there is a ready-made checklist of performance standards and criteria for you to use. By investing an hour or two discussing these with your local college of further education or other training provided you could save yourself a lot of effort.

Skills-, knowledge- and attitude-based objectives

As we saw earlier in this chapter, not all training needs revolve around competencies. Some relate directly to the *knowledge* and understanding that underpins behaviour. Others reflect the acquisition of the basic *skills* that underlie specific competencies. Competency-based objectives are normally expressed in terms of what the learner will be able to *do* afterwards, and to what standard. For example:

> At the end of the session the learner will be able to structure a training and development session which receives positive evaluation ratings from all participants and their managers at a four-week follow-up.

Knowledge-based objectives are more likely to be couched in terms of what the learner will *understand and be able to explain or describe*. For example:

> At the end of the session the learner will be able to explain the main purpose of establishing learning objectives before designing a training event.

Skills-based objectives are, like competency-based ones, likely to be phrased in terms of what the learner will be able to do after training, but the context in which he or she is expected to do it may be less specific. A skill-based objective for Audrey in the example above might be:

> At the end of the session the learner will be able to operate a keyboard at 50 words a minute.

Where individual *attitudes* are concerned, matters must be approached with particular sensitivity. If someone is either consciously or unconsciously choosing not to do his or her best, the reasons must be understood – not least by the person himself or herself. It could be that he or she feels undervalued in their present role. If so, training could be a way of showing that he or she *is* valued. But it must be the right kind of training or it will have the opposite effect.

Alternatively, he or she may already feel or be over-qualified for the job and be disinclined to make an effort – without realising that he or she is doing a bad job. In that case, training may be quite the wrong solution. Instead, you may need to help him or her to come to terms with the situation, or to find a role more suited to his or her talents!

Coaching to define objectives

Your task as a trainer is to help line managers and prospective trainees be as precise as possible. A simple 'What do you want him/her to be able to do after the training?' is likely to get you an unhelpful 'A better job.' Instead, you must establish:

- what the manager and employee see as their goal – what they are trying to achieve through training
- what success will look like, how success will be measured by them
- where they stand now in relation to the goal – how far short of 10 out of 10
- where and when they first became aware of the gap, in what circumstances, who else was involved, what was happening, whether there were particular time constraints or financial issues, how often it has been an issue, and if there have been instances when it has *not* been an issue.

Once you have coached them through to this point, there is a possibility that the training need will disappear! Either of two reasons could explain this.

- They have decided it is not worth the effort of trying to persuade you that a need exists – or, more positively,
- The coaching process through which you have taken them will have raised their awareness of when and how the problem arises – and hence how to solve it.

The trainer who suspects that the first applies will need to probe carefully, continuing the coaching process by asking

- what solutions have already been tried, and with what effects
- what options there are now
- how each would impact on the goal.

It may be that a solution other than formal training will emerge. If so, you will have done your job. If there *is* still a need for training, at least you will all, by now, have a very clear picture of its real objectives and can plan accordingly.

This sort of cross-examination of people whom you probably think of as your customers may not quite fit with your (or their) expectations of the training role. But as we shall see in Chapter 11, the role of the trainer is increasingly that of internal consultant. Among other things, that means helping people to help themselves, rather than doing things for them.

DEVELOPING A TRAINING PLAN

Once the research and analysis process and the definition of objectives are complete, you can start planning how to tackle each of the needs to meet the objectives that have emerged. This may be done at individual, group or whole organisation level, and often builds up from one to the other. An organisation-wide training plan must reflect needs at each of the three levels.

Its precise contents will vary according to the requirements of senior management. If it is to help senior management assess priorities – see Chapter 10 – and provide a basis for measuring the effectiveness of the training function – Chapter 9 – it should at least identify

- the numbers to be trained
- the competencies to be developed/the objectives to be met
- the duration of training
- the anticipated costs.

Formulating the plan will tend to be an iterative process, because

- the identification of needs and numbers may take some time in a large organisation
- once the needs have been identified and precise objectives formulated, the options with regard to possible training solutions will have to be researched and costed
- a timetable of events must be prepared – and one that does not conflict with the operational needs of the organisation or the team.

As a start point, once individual learning objectives have been defined, you will have the basis of an individual learning plan. Below is a pro forma for recording this, although there are many proprietary HR and training systems which will allow you to input the information into a training database. Chapters 3 to 6 help identify the methods to use. Chapter 9 gives guidance on evaluation.

Individual training plan (pro forma)

Name: ....

Subject: ....

Date: ....

Objectives
(What the employee should be able to do as a result of the activity)
....
....

Expected outcomes
(How the training will improve knowledge/skills and improve job performance)
....
....

Present skill level
(Level of skill and/or previous experience within subject)
....

Main content and methods
(Syllabus, skill areas and method – ie lecture, video, experiential, etc)
....
....

How and when learning activity will take place

Location ....

Date(s) ....

Time ....

Total cost   Course fee ....

                        Time ....

                        Subsistence ....

Using this documentation will not only help you and the trainee to focus on what is to be done, it will also provide a basis for your record of what has been done. This is important. If your organisation hopes to be recognised as an Investor in People (Chapter 1) you will need to prove that training is both planned and delivered.

The plans for each individual can be brought together to make sure that the most cost-effective training solutions are found. If there are several people with the same need, it may be more cost-effective and beneficial for them to do their learning together rather than separately. Table 13 is a pro forma on which the group or organisation plan can be brought together. The options for learning methods, providers and locations are examined in the next two chapters, and budgeting is considered in Chapter 10.

Table 13   *Outline combined training plan*

Date	Course	Duration	Total hours	Delegates	Total cost

SUMMARY: QUICK TIPS

- Individual employees, groups and the whole organisation need to
  - ensure that work is done to appropriate standards
  - continuously improve
  - set new, more stretching goals and objectives to move forward.
- When identifying learning needs at each of these levels, it is important to watch for conflicts and inconsistencies between each level of need.
- Choose the method(s) of identifying learning needs that will get you enough information to make sure you understand the real need and can formulate a learning objective that the employee and the line manager can both recognise and buy in to.
- Involve senior management, line managers, customers and intended participants in your analysis of learning needs, through interview, observation and faults analysis as well as performance appraisal and development centres.
- Keep careful notes of your interviews and analyses. You may need to re-visit them later to check out whether training has had the desired effect.
- Convert your ideas into specific, measurable objectives that are competency-based.
  - Remember that the definition of *competencies* can provide a useful framework for establishing behaviourally-based objectives. These are usually expressed in terms of the things the learner will be able to do afterwards.
  - Defining objectives is easier where there are clearly defined *performance indicators* and *standards of performance.*
  - Sometimes it will be appropriate to dig a little deeper, to identify the underlying *skills* and *knowledge* which will enable competency to develop. Where this is the case, objectives will be phrased in terms of what the learner will be able to understand and explain or the basic skills he or she will be able to demonstrate.
  - The role of *attitudes* in learning is an important one. Sometimes it will be necessary to design training with the specific objective of changing people's *beliefs* about what is, or is not, appropriate behaviour.

- The trainer's task is to consult with all those who may be able to help define learning objectives, and to coach line managers and potential learners to make sure that the objectives are clear and fully understood by all concerned.

■ Build your individual training plan into one for the whole section or organisation.

■ Be realistic: if your organisation or some of the people in it are not fully committed to training, you will need some 'quick wins' to prove its effectiveness. Make sure you reflect this in your training plans.

Individual task

■ Work with a colleague to practise the sort of questions which will help you to define learning objectives.

■ Ask him or her to choose something about which he or she would like to know more or be better at.

■ Then probe to find out
  - what he or she sees as the ultimate goal
  - what success will look like, how he or she will measure it
  - where he or she stands now in relation to the goal – how far short of 10 out of 10
  - where and when he or she first became aware of the gap, in what circumstances, who else was involved, what was happening, whether there were particular time constraints or financial issues, how often it has been an issue
  - if there have been instances where it has *not* been an issue.

Choosing appropriate learning opportunities

ON-THE-JOB VERSUS OFF-THE-JOB LEARNING

The process of establishing learning objectives should help pinpoint the best way of meeting them. The choice will depend on:

- the organisation's training policy
- the precise need to be met
- the urgency of the need
- the resources (time, skills and equipment) available inside the organisation, and their location
- the resources available outside the organisation
- the state of the training budget – see Chapter 10.

On-the-job learning

On-the-job learning is not always conscious or structured. Personal reflection on what seems to work/please the boss/satisfy the customer leads people to try alternatives and modify their behaviour without external support. Providing diaries can foster this spontaneous movement around the learning cycle, and learning logs – see Chapter 11 – can encourage reflection. In some organisations, self-coaching increases the benefits to be gained.

On-the-job learning is not restricted to the learner's own current job. Job rotation, work shadowing or secondments to other parts of the business can broaden the chance for learning. Special projects can provide further learning opportunities within a job.

Understanding on-the-job learning as learning that takes place in the learners' normal workplace in the course of doing their work, it is clear that the label can cover a multitude of approaches: everything from 'sink or swim' and 'learn by your mistakes' via the traditional 'sit next to Nelly' or a more formal 'buddy system' to a carefully planned programme of on-the-job coaching, working through the elements of the task in logical sequence with a skilled coach. Each method may have something to offer, depending on circumstances. All will benefit from being used in a planned and controlled way.

The art lies in

- identifying the level of support the learner will need, when
- working out who can give it.

Sometimes it may be appropriate to let an individual or team work through a particular project or piece of work without much help – and then review the whole thing at the end to draw out and help reinforce learning. Sometimes it may be better to have someone working alongside who can provide minute-by-minute coaching and support.

Clearly, where questions of safety are involved, a novice must never be left alone to work out the best way of operating dangerous equipment. Elsewhere, a small amount of initial coaching, followed by review sessions at key points, can work well. In general, for learning to be effective it helps if there is careful distinction between tasks which must be done in a prescribed manner in order to produce the required quality or speed of output, and tasks for which employees are free to use their own initiative.

For tasks in the first category, it may be necessary to devote some effort to producing a clear and logical step-by-step procedure so that learners can refer to it as they work.

Alternatively, and potentially more effectively, someone can coach the learner from first principles. If the steps needed to complete the task are logical, the learner should be able to work them out – and remember them as a result. The coach must

- identify a logical place to start. For some tasks it is possible to allow learners to experiment – to 'find out what happens if I press this key or pull that lever'. For others it could be disastrous. Then it would be better to ask the learners to think about what the machine is designed to do, what control they will need over it, and so on
- observe the learners, and ask questions to help raise awareness. If they each focus on 'what I notice when I do this', adjustments to posture, grip, tension, and so on will tend to follow until it feels right. The approach is explained in more detail later in Chapter 4.

Usually the person best placed to give this sort of coaching is someone who works closely with the individual. He or she will not need to set up special sessions or familiarise himself or herself with the work process, and he or she will probably be in a position to carry on coaching throughout the working day.

Whoever does it, it is important to focus on asking questions and encouraging the learners to think and try for themselves, rather than just telling or showing them how to do it. It will also of course be vital to recognise when a trainee is performing to the required standard. If learning is directed towards achieving an NVQ as well as satisfactory job performance, someone must assess whether the right level of competence has been reached.

> **The benefits of on-the-job learning**
>
> - Training is carried out in the same circumstances as the job itself. The trainee should have no problem in seeing the relevance of what is being learnt, or in transferring it back to the job.
> - Training can more readily be provided on a just-in-time basis, exactly when needed, rather than at predetermined times.
> - There may be less need for special equipment/materials to be provided. Depending on safety and output considerations, it may be possible to use operational resources.

Some of the key questions when contemplating on-the-job learning are:

- Is the training properly planned?
- Will enough time and resources be devoted to it?
- Will it be properly documented to prove that training has taken place?
- Will it be conducted by an effective coach?
- Has proper account been taken of any health or safety hazards?
- Will competence be assessed fairly and accurately?
- Will it be carefully evaluated ?

Off-the-job learning

Off-the-job learning may be the only way to acquire the background knowledge needed for some jobs. Indeed, relevant off-the-job learning, in the form of academic study or vocational training, is likely to form part of the employee specification for recruitment. Beyond that, it is often necessary to make sure that people know the basics, the underlying theories or legislation governing particular types of work. It may also be the only safe way to allow learners to practise skills or develop competence without slowing output or reducing quality. It might, for instance, be risky to allow a customer service representative to practise on real customers before he or she has learnt a bit about the organisation's policy and how to demonstrate its products to best effect.

Off-the-job training can be carried out one-to-one by the learner's own boss or colleagues – simply using space and equipment away from the normal workplace. It can also take the form of reading, computer-based learning or other types of solo study – see Chapter 5. Often, it implies bringing together a number of employees with similar needs away from their desks or workbenches.

TAUGHT VERSUS DISTANCE LEARNING

That learning takes place away from the job does not have to mean attendance at a training course. Nor does it have to mean that a trainer must be present throughout. An increasing proportion of all learning is now being done via technology and/or books and manuals. In fact, learning can take place anywhere along the continuum shown in Figure 3.

Model A will be familiar to many as the conventional school/college model. Interaction with the trainer is regular and frequent. Although parts of the learning process can include 'homework', this is very much as an adjunct to the main taught programme in which all the learners come together to share their learning activities.

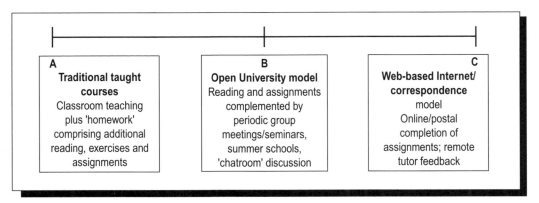

Figure 3 *The teaching continuum*

Model B represents the established pattern of distance learning. The tutor or trainer is still important, as a guide to the learning process and the provider of feedback about performance. Face-to-face meetings with other learners are much less frequent. They do occur, both as a formal part of the programme and informally – when two or more like-minded learners meet, write, phone or e-mail each other to compare notes on particular topics or to get the feel of how they are doing relative to others.

Model C is where all encounters between learners and between learner and tutor are remotely conducted – via e-mail or other forms of correspondence. Learning takes place via reading or exercises or simulations in which the learner can participate from home or the workplace. Feedback comes either electronically or via written comments from the tutor/trainer. Some of the advantages and disadvantages of the three models are summed up in Table 14.

None of the three models, or variations on the continuum between them, is intrinsically good or bad. Each has its potential uses. In determining which to use to meet a particular learning need or set of needs, consider:

- the availability of established and proven programmes
- the number of people to be trained
- the geographical locations and spread of the people to be trained
- the type of skills/knowledge/competency to be learned
- the value to be added by allowing trainees to meet face to face and develop their social and organisational networks
- the relative costs
- the importance of making sure that everyone moves at the same pace and/or finishes at the same time
- the availability of the appropriate resources – tutors/trainers, computers, course materials, Internet access, etc.

Although cost is usually a key consideration, often the first and last of these will be the deciding factors. Sometimes it may be possible to get the best of both worlds through a combination of approaches.

Table 14 *Taught versus distance learning*

Model A – mainly taught	Model B – mixed	Model C – all remote
	Advantages for the learner	
Tutor/trainer can respond to range of learning styles	Some opportunities to respond to individual styles	More sophisticated packages cater for all styles
Chance to mix and learn from others	Occasional chances to mix	No travelling time/costs
Assignments test and reinforce learning	Assignments test and reinforce learning	Assignments test and reinforce learning
Tutor/trainer is available and may be seen as more approachable	Some opportunity to work at own pace	Work at own pace
Requirement for regular attendance can help to sustain motivation	Greater flexibility over when and where to study	Full flexibility over when and where to study
	Advantages for the organisation	
Easy to make sure everyone is still participating. Non-attenders conspicuous and can be chased	Added flexibility; less time away from work; useful if employees are geographically dispersed	Complete flexibility; may be no need for time away from work; no travel time or costs
Finite length of programme makes monitoring and evaluation easier	Regular meetings allow for progress checking and monitoring	Can be very cost-effective
	Disadvantages for the learner	
Rigid timings and set locations limit flexibility	Motivation may flag between meetings	Very high level of self-motivation and self-discipline essential
Group and/or tutor/trainer may not 'gel'	Variable amount/quality of tutor/trainer support	Variable quality of materials
Pace may be too fast or too slow	Variable accessibility of tutor/trainer	Learning often too generic to meet specific need (see Chapter 11)
		Lack of personal tutor/trainer support and guidance
	Disadvantages for the organisation	
May be driven by trainer availability not employee need – may not be best use of resources	Relatively high cost to develop in-house	Very high cost to develop in-house
May be disproportionate amounts of travel and social time	Some learners may fall too far behind between meetings and be unable to catch up	Off-the-shelf packages lack organisation/job context
Set length of course may mean too much (or too little) time devoted to particular topics	'Soft'/interpersonal skills tend to be crammed into group sessions	May not be as effective in developing 'soft'/interpersonal skills as face-to-face methods
		Possible high drop-out rate

THE ROLE OF TECHNOLOGY

In Chapter 11 some current debates about the future role of technology are explored. Here we provide a more general overview of its current contribution.

Information and learning technology (ILT) takes a number of forms. These include:

- video and DVD packages, covering a very wide range of topics and distributed by specialist production companies
- CD-ROM which can be used with any PC that has an appropriate disk drive
- information freely accessible on the Internet via common search-engines or at known websites
- training packages accessed via the Internet (usually on payment of a fee/subscription) – these include materials from both private providers and *learndirect*, the government-sponsored provider whose materials can be accessed from special University for Industry (UfI) access points in colleges, libraries and other places open to the public. You can find out more at www.learndirect.co.uk
- e-mail, which can be used to send and receive information to and from a training provider or between learners.

The last three are increasingly referred to as 'e-learning'. Where ILT is used as a substitute for classroom activity, it can have a number of the advantages listed for Model C in Table 14. More specifically, the learner can usually

- decide when to switch on
- decide when to switch off
- fast-forward to move ahead
- go back to key points
- test out what happens when the wrong answer is given
- find out what happens when the right answer is given
- ask for help when needed.

In short, with the more advanced packages, the learner has a completely flexible, all-knowing tutor at the touch of a key or the click of a mouse button. With CD-ROM it is possible to check things out from a number of different angles – see the video, hear the soundtrack, watch the screen, answer the questions and get truly involved with the learning process. Well-designed technology-based training has many advantages.

- It is stimulating and involving.
- It takes learners right around the learning cycle.
- It can be used time and again by the same or different employees.
- It is quick and easy to learn to use.

For many learners, this sounds like the ideal solution. It means they can follow their own interests and work at their own pace. But for some – especially those who still suffer from 'technophobia' (fear of technology) – it may be less appealing. It also has the disadvantage of being relatively expensive to produce and the range of products on offer is still limited and of variable quality. It may also leave the learner a little too free to determine the pace. Although some packages do record progress and test learning, that has a 'big brother is watching you' connotation that makes some trainers and learners uncomfortable.

Many larger organisations have established their own technology-based learning centres, often on an open-access basis. That means that employees from any part of the organisation can simply book in or turn up during their lunchbreak or after work to use the facilities – whether or not the learning is relevant to their job. Fords, for example, make the facilities available to the local community as well as their own employees.

TRAINING PROVIDERS

Your own organisation's employees can deliver both on-the-job and off-the-job training. Often this will be the best route to ensure that all learning is relevant to the organisation and its working methods and standards. Sometimes, though, you will need someone trained in new skills not already available within the organisation. Sometimes lack of time and/or training expertise may point you in the direction of outside suppliers.

In some instances the choice of training provider may precede the choice of a specific method. The provider may be the best judge of how to meet the objectives. In other cases, the type of approach required will be an internal decision, and a supplier with expertise in using it will then be selected.

External sources

These divide broadly into public and private training providers. Your local college of further education receives much of its funding from the LSC (see Chapter 1) and is in a position to draw down money to subsidise training for vocational qualifications and other learning. It will almost certainly be able to offer a range of very practical courses – from welding to beauty therapy and from software engineering to childcare. Most lead either to an NVQ or to other qualifications recognised by the industry, and cover all levels from foundation to professional.

Even if you do not require your employees to be formally qualified, the college may be able to tailor a short course specifically for you, perhaps finding other local employers with similar needs to share the costs. Although this route is relatively more expensive in cash terms, the savings in employee time may make it more attractive. You will find the college address and telephone number in the telephone directory. At more senior levels, universities and institutes of higher education can provide a similar service.

The issues to consider in choosing a supplier include:

- reputation – does the supplier have a good name for delivering what it promises?
- the skills and resources offered
- cost
- the geographical location
- availability at the required time.

The overriding consideration is of course proficiency in achieving the required learning objectives. You will have to choose between those who specialise in a particular area and those who offer a wider portfolio. If, for example, the need is for someone to provide telephone skills training, your choice might be between

- the business unit at your local college
- a specialist local consultant
- the supplier of your telephone hardware
- another telephone company
- a company specialising in communications training

- a company offering office and administrative training
- a company with a complete portfolio of managerial, administrative and clerical courses
- an information-technology-based solution provided by one of the above or a specialist.

To help find your way around the large array of providers, both public and private, the government has launched a new national *learndirect* telephone helpline. The telephone number is 0800 100 900. This offers free information and advice on learning opportunities for adults at all levels and all disciplines – from hobbies through to PhD. Alternatively, visit the website at www.learndirect.co.uk

It is important to make sure that your chosen supplier will work to the standards and in the manner you require. For instance, not all providers have monitoring processes to guarantee that trainees actually do attend. This may occasionally be a problem where, for instance, you provide day-release to attend a course and the learner unilaterally decides that there are better things to do on a Wednesday afternoon. Since day-release courses generally lead to qualifications of some kind, you may be tolerant and reckon that the end justifies the means. If the qualification is achieved, it is up to trainees to decide how best to allocate their time. Others take a less lenient view and insist that the course provider notify them of any absence so it can be tackled immediately.

It is worth taking time and trouble to choose the right provider – not only because of the direct costs involved but also because inappropriate or ineffective training may put people off the whole idea of training for the future. The steps involved are:

1   Research the options – this could involve contacting *learndirect*, trawling web- or paper-based directories and brochures, then telephone-calls followed by meetings with a shortlist of possible providers and/or third-party sources like the LSC to establish their track record.
2   Consider the wider issues – if the proposed training is only the first step in a larger training plan, it may make sense to start working with someone who will be able to contribute more later – reducing the amount of familiarisation time that will be needed before subsequent stages. Against this must be weighed the issue of trainer credibility. While familiarity will save time, having the same so-called 'specialist' popping up on six different subjects may stretch the credulity of trainees.
3   Clarify the detail – just what is the provider offering to do, when, where, for how many trainees, over how long a period, at what cost, with what learning methods and with what guarantees of success?
4   Apply your selection criteria as objectively as possible.

Internal sources

If you do have the resources to do the training in-house, it is still important to think through which of a number of possible trainers should be nominated to help achieve particular learning objectives. The factors to be considered include:

- subject expertise
- coaching skills
- commitment to helping others learn
- competence in using relevant learning methods
- credibility with trainees
- availability – at the times and in the locations where training will take place.

Sometimes there is only one possible contender. Sometimes you will be faced with a choice – perhaps between the 'subject expert' and the potentially more effective 'coach'.

OPEN VERSUS TAILORED TRAINING

Open – or public – training is, in its purest sense, available to all comers – ie to any company or part of a company that wishes to nominate delegates. Tailored training is designed to meet the specific needs of a particular organisation or part of it.

The terms are most frequently used in the context of external provision. Here, truly open courses are those for which there are no entry requirements beyond the ability to find the course fee. Pre-screening of delegates is limited, although the more reputable providers do their best to prevent any major mismatches between delegate and trainer expectations.

Open courses may be offered, via prospectuses, mailshots, training indexes and data bases, several times a year. The provider generally tries to give a reasonable insight into the objectives, content, methods and target audience for the course. There is usually an upper and lower limit on the number of delegates. This can be useful to know. Too few delegates can be just as counter-productive as too many, unless the learning methods are adapted accordingly. The training provider who simply reduces the amount of trainer support to keep costs down and protect profit margins is not necessarily doing your learners any favours.

The process of nominating, briefing and debriefing delegates for open training is likely to be slightly different from that for tailored or in-house training. Particularly careful evaluation is needed to help build a register of 'approved suppliers' – those courses and providers who are worth using again. The advantages and disadvantages of open courses include those listed in Table 15.

Table 15 *Advantages and disadvantages of open courses*

Advantages	Disadvantages
Learners are exposed to people from other organisations, which can help to broaden their perspectives	The presence of delegates from many different types of organisation with differing needs can be a distraction – and may occasionally lead to disenchantment with the learner's own organisation
The provider may be able to pull together specialists in particular subject areas to provide a more rounded programme than would be possible otherwise	Because learning is not organisation-specific, learners, and their bosses, must critically assess which parts of the learning really fit back in the workplace
The costs per head may be lower than for comparable tailored programmes because development costs can be spread across several courses	Sometimes people will be overly critical of the 'academic' theory learnt, dismissing it as irrelevant to the real world. Sometimes learners will uncritically accept that principles and practices they have been taught must apply in their entirety, without recognising the differences in objectives, structure, climate, work processes, relationships and other factors in their own organisation. This can mean that transplanting ideas can be just as accident-prone as any other kind of transplant. Unless the ground is well prepared and the climate conducive, it may be better not to try

It is not only courses that can be open or tailored. The costs of developing and producing books, videos, computer-based training and interactive multimedia programmes often have to be shared between a number of people if they are to be offered at affordable prices. Although not all the advantages and disadvantages apply in the same way, the problem of applying the general principles they contain in the specific context in which learners are working is a continuing issue. For this reason, the idea of working in partnership with one or more providers to customise an existing programme or design one from scratch can be attractive.

Tailored training is more commonly a feature in larger organisations where there are significant numbers of people with the same or similar learning needs. That way the development costs can be spread. But even in quite a small firm there may be occasions when it would be better for a number of people to be trained together. Work to involve everyone in the identification of key results areas, or the introduction of a major new proficiency requirement, are just two examples.

Working with providers to create tailored training means that a partnership must be developed. This entails:

- establishing clear goals and ways of measuring results and progress: the specific learning objectives will be one input, but there may be others – such as prototyping the methodology or creating an in-house capability to deliver future programmes
- setting up a 'project plan' to identify the tasks to be completed in the design, testing, administration, delivery and evaluation of the programme – with critical deadlines and milestones
- clarifying roles and responsibilities at the outset, setting out exactly who will do what, when
- monitoring progress regularly to ensure that deadlines and quality targets are met.

In addition, it may be necessary to

- set up a mutual familiarisation programme, to enable outsiders to understand your organisation and its goals for the project
- make sure that the providers have access to all the people and information they need
- review the drafts of content, exercises, tests and other components to make sure that their style, language, level, and the messages they contain are compatible with the needs and style of your organisation.

THE ACCREDITATION OF LEARNING

The role of the Awarding Bodies and the QCA was explained in Chapter 1. If you think that some of the training provided, either internally or externally, would be enhanced by external accreditation, it would be worth discussing the matter either with the provider (if external) or with your local college of further education, university or Institute of Higher Education.

The main advantages are that:

- there will be objective assessment of the standard reached by the learners which can be linked to pay or other forms of recognition or career progression
- learners' self-esteem may be enhanced by acquiring formal recognition of their skills
- the credibility of the training and its value may be enhanced
- learners may feel more loyalty to an organisation that has invested in them in this way

- if the organisation needs to make employees redundant, learners with qualifications are more likely to find new work quickly.

The main disadvantages are likely to be:

- cost
- potential distortion of the learning programme to include aspects required to meet Awarding Body requirements rather than organisational needs
- qualified employees will be more marketable and may be poached by other employers.

SUMMARY: QUICK TIPS

In choosing who to engage to help learners meet the objectives you have identified,

- Weigh up the relevance and benefits of off-the-job versus on-the-job training.
- Consider whether learning would be helped by bringing learners together for a 'taught' element, in whatever way that is to be delivered.
- Assess whether technology could assist in or provide the means of delivery.
- Think whether anyone inside the organisation has the credibility, expertise and other attributes necessary to deliver the programme or whether you would do better to look externally.
- Weigh up whether to enrol people on an open programme in which they will mingle with learners from other organisations (either in reality or via supporting Internet chatrooms).
- Decide whether it is the type of learning to which value will be added, for the learner and the organisation, by acquiring external accreditation so that learners obtain a recognised qualification.

Designing training

CHAPTER 4

CHAPTER OBJECTIVES

When you have read this chapter you should be able to:

■ list at least four factors which should influence the design of training

■ list at least eight different training methods and give an example of a learning objective for each

■ identify at least three factors which should influence the structure of a training session

■ explain what is meant by 'transfer of learning' and how it can be encouraged in the workplace.

PREPARATION

Clarity of objectives (see Chapter 2) is the first essential for effective training. Unless you know what the learners are to be able to do at the end of the session, your training design may be intellectually pleasing but totally useless.

Once the objectives are clear, there are still a number of other factors that should influence the choice of methods and the sequence in which they are used – that is, the design of the training event(s).

These factors include:

■ the learning styles of those to be trained (see the first section of Chapter 1) – the use of a variety of methods to reinforce the same objectives is desirable, to cater to as many learning styles as possible

■ the number of learners. Some of the methods described in *Choosing the method* below require a minimum number to be effective. In role-play, for example, the group will need to be big enough to enable all the required roles to be filled, with some left to observe the interaction and provide feedback. Maximum numbers will depend on the time and resources available. A large number of groups or 'cells' of learners may all be taken through a programme in parallel, provided that all the materials and facilitation aids can be replicated for each cell. Some very ambitious parallel activities have proved successful – including the induction and customer-care training of all the staff employed at the Millennium Dome. The basic rule on numbers is that they should recognise that learning is an active process. Too large a group and too little individual involvement or attention from the trainer can lead to learners getting lost

■ location, resources and facilities. In the real world, trainers must to some extent cut their coat according to their cloth. The ingenious trainer will never let an imperfect room layout or poor facilities impact adversely on learning outcomes, and will certainly not draw attention to them or blame them for the quality of the learning experience. Nevertheless, if all you have is a room with fixed seating and no projection facilities, the range of methods open to you is considerably less than if you had a choice of rooms and outdoor spaces, with flexible seating and a range of visual display methods

■ time may also be a limiting factor. Judging the right pace for training is not easy, and the difficulties will be compounded if, for example, you find yourself running out of time towards the end of a session or, conversely, running out of material half-way through the allotted timespan. Many new trainers seriously underestimate the length of time it can take to get a group of learners to switch from one learning method to another. After half an hour's listening, the casual conversation, comfort-breaks and requests for repeat explanations of the brief can mean that it takes several minutes to move from, for example, an input session into discussion groups.

Effective design is about more than choosing methods to suit objectives, learning styles and resources. The sequencing of material can also be critical. Where prior knowledge or skill is needed to enable new learning to take place, or to take place safely, this must be taken into account. Obvious examples relate to advanced IT applications with which learners who lack basic IT skills will not get to grips, or machine operations which demand the ability to start, stop and control the machine as the first step. Training electricians to fit a switch before they understand wiring and current is just one of thousands of potentially lethal sequencing faults. The pro forma for an individual training plan given in Chapter 2 (page 46) will help you to plan training with these factors in mind.

CHOOSING THE METHOD

Wherever and by whom training is to be conducted, careful thought must be given to the method to be employed. The choice can be divided into three broad categories:

■ trainer-centred training
■ learner-centred training
■ coaching.

Trainer-centred training

Trainer-centred training gives the trainer control over the pace and content of learning. Lectures/presentations and demonstrations are the most obviously trainer-centred methods. The trainer decides the content and delivers it at the pace he or she thinks appropriate. The learners can, of course, slow things down – by asking lots of questions or misbehaving. They are less likely to be able to speed things up – at least in the short term. They do still have some choices to make – to listen or not, to ask questions or not. But the trainer sets the pace.

Role-plays, where for example the trainer pretends to be a customer and asks the trainee to serve him or her or handle a 'complaint', are more participative. So too are practical exercises. Trainees can determine the pace a little more. But it is generally the trainer who decides which role-plays or exercises to use. And it is likely to be the trainer who sets the timetable, structures the debriefing session and draws out the key learning points.

Learner-centred training

At the other extreme are methods which give the learner more or less complete control. Among long-established learner-centred methods are printed books and journals and self-study texts. Self-development questionnaires, personal learning logs and other such tools provide scope for more active learning. The various forms of technology-based learning outlined in Chapter 3 are also generally designed to be learner-centred.

Coaching

This is the only method that really allows trainer and learner to develop a learning partnership and to share control. In essence it involves:

- identifying a clear, challenging yet realistic goal or learning objective. This should be something the learner wants to achieve rather than being dictated by the trainer – although it must be set in the context of the overall objectives of the training programme

- raising awareness of where the learner currently really stands in relation to the goal, and of when, where, how often and in what circumstances it is an issue. The coach asks the questions. In searching for the answers the learner becomes more aware of the reality of how he or she is approaching the task at present and begins to identify some possible directions for change

- identifying options – the things the learner could do to get nearer the goal. Initially, all the ideas should come from the learner without any attempt to evaluate them or decide which to adopt. The trainer's ideas do not form part of the process unless the learner asks for suggestions. Only when all the learner's ideas have been listed may the coach ask the learner to begin to weigh up the possibilities

- working through each option to see how it might help and what it would take to make it work; determining which action the learner will take. This normally emerges quite spontaneously as the learner narrows down the options

- pinning down exactly what the learner will do, by when, what help is needed, what obstacles must be overcome, and how that will be done.

Because the coach is there, asking questions and listening attentively to the replies, learners should never feel isolated or left to their own devices. Because the learner is totally involved in setting the goal and answering the questions, the trainer need never fear that the learner has switched off or lost interest.

Coaching can be used with teams, groups or individuals. It can also be used as a general problem-solving process. The basic principles of questioning and the model of working through the four key steps (GROW) of:

- goal
- reality
- options
- will

hold in all these contexts. It is therefore one of the key skills – perhaps *the* key skill – for anyone seeking to help other people learn. The process is explained in detail by John Whitmore in his book *Coaching for Performance*.

Table 16 describes some of the most frequently used learning methods and indicates

- the type of learning outcomes to which each is potentially most suited
- whether it is essentially a learner-centred or trainer-centred method.

Table 16 *Learning methods*

Method	Description	Usual outcome	Trainer- or learner- centred
Lectures and presentations	Trainer delivers prepared exposition, preferably using visual aids	Knowledge – facts and opinions	Trainer
Briefing groups	Short exposition by trainer, followed by questions and discussion	Knowledge – facts and opinions	Mainly trainer
Discussion groups	Participative discussion led by one of the learners, on a specified topic	Some knowledge – facts and opinions; also attitudes and interpersonal skills	Mainly trainer
Plenary discussion	Session following practical or other activity, usually led by the trainer to pull out key learning points and/or relate theory to practice	Reinforcement and reflection – depends on task under review	Mainly trainer
Demonstrations	Trainer shows learners how to eg operate machine, conduct an interview	Knowledge – how to; preparation for skills training	Trainer
Practicals	Learners operate under trainer's supervision and receive feedback	Psychomotor or inter-personal skills	Trainer
Role-play	Learners put themselves in someone else's shoes for the purpose of practical exercise	Changing attitudes; interpersonal skills eg interviewing, negotiating, customer care	Trainer
Pre-recorded video/DVD	Sound and vision	Knowledge – how to; preparation for skills training	Trainer
Case studies	Write-up of an incident or situation, with questions for analysis and/or discussion	Analytical and decision-making skills; some inter-personal skills if done in groups	Mainly trainer
Business games/computer simulations	Board or computer games or evolving case studies which allow participants to see the consequences of their decisions	Analytical and decision-making skills; some inter-personal skills if done in groups	Mainly trainer
Incident method	Learners are given last item in a sequence of events and asked to reconstruct circumstances through questioning trainer	Analytical and questioning skills	Trainer
Team tasks	Practical indoor or outdoor exercises or simulations	Planning, organising, team and interpersonal skills	Possibly both, depending on style of debriefing

Table 16 *Continued*

Method	Description	Usual outcome	Trainer- or learner- centred
In-tray exercises	Learners are given a series of memos and other papers or electronic communications, to be prioritised and dealt with	Prioritising, planning, organising, delegating and other managerial skills	Trainer
Group/individual projects	Investigation and report, usually with recommendations, on issues of concern	Knowledge – facts and opinions; investigative, analytical and problem-solving skills; some inter-personal skills, especially for group projects	Mainly learner
Books, manuals and self-study texts	Written descriptions, analyses or instructions, sometimes with checklists and self-test questions	Knowledge – facts and opinions; preparation for skills training	Learner
e-learning	Electronic, Internet-based media which present learner with information and/or situations and questions and provide feedback on responses	Most except practical inter-personal skills	Learner
Embedded e-learning	Computer 'trains' the operator step by step as tasks are carried out	Knowledge and skills, but varying extent of actual learning	Learner
Learning log	Diary or journal used by learner to reflect on work or learning events and draw out and record learning points	All types	Learner
Coaching	Learner takes responsibility for own learning and uses trainer as coach to raise awareness	All types	Both

STRUCTURING A SESSION

Once you have identified the objectives and the methods to be used, the structure of the session itself will begin to emerge. There are five main factors to consider:

- the learning cycle
- logical flow
- variation
- duration
- assessment and evaluation.

The learning cycle

We saw in Chapter 1 how this should influence your design. Much will depend on where the learners are starting from. If they already have practical experience of the topic, and if there are reflectors in the group, you might start with a question-and-answer session or a group discussion geared to reflecting what they have already observed. You might then get them to formulate their own 'theory' – for example, a list of the circumstances in which particular action or behaviour might be appropriate or where the same set of outcomes might be expected. They can test this out in a further practical session.

Alternatively, you may decide to start with an activity, to get the learners (particularly the activists) involved and interested and move on around the cycle with a more reflective, discussion phase. When you draw the outcomes together you can challenge the learners to relate their conclusions to underpinning concepts or theories.

Logical flow

Frequent switches of method will confuse learners, especially if each presents a different angle on the same topic. Using one method – a simulation or role-play perhaps – and then the coaching framework to guide the debriefing will be less confusing than trying to pack in a wide variety in a short time-frame.

Variation

Although it is important to avoid 'bittyness', it is also important to vary the methods used. The maximum attention span for presentations is about 20 minutes. Even with interesting visual aids (see Chapter 5) and some interruptions for questions and answers, unalleviated input is not likely to retain the attention of the learners. A flow of activity, moving naturally around the learning cycle to reinforce and extend learning is likely to be more effective.

Duration

For sessions lasting a whole day or longer, the range and variety of methods to be introduced will be far wider than for short, one- or two-hour sessions. If training has to be broken down into a number of short bursts, it will be particularly important to keep momentum going between sessions – perhaps through self-study or distance learning. Even so, the first part of each session may have to be taken up with some sort of rehearsal of the work that has gone before. Unless a period back at work can be used as an integral part of the learning process, it will usually be better to opt for fewer, longer sessions with scope for more variety in each.

Assessment and evaluation

Incorporating some means of assessing learners' progress into your design is essential. Without it, the trainer cannot gauge the pace of the training. There is then a risk that

- learners will not be stretched and challenged and may become bored and frustrated, or
- the pace will be too fast and some or all the learners will become confused, unable to reach the required objective, or dispirited and again frustrated.

One of the quickest and easiest methods of assessing progress during the session is via questions and answers. Questions may be addressed either to selected individuals or to the whole group. They can also be

- direct – eg 'What is the key promise that we make to our customers?' or 'Which combination of keys would you press to cut and paste a sentence?' – to which there is a definite and usually fairly brief answer, or

- open – eg 'What do you think will happen if I press this lever now?', which may require a longer description in reply. We consider questions and how to handle them in more detail in Chapter 6.

We explore more formal methods of post-course assessment in Chapter 7. Within the session itself, apart from asking questions, the two main options are:

- observation
- test.

Observation

Set a task and watch how well the learners cope with it. If they struggle, they may need some reinforcement of earlier learning.

Test

Again a task can be set, but rather than monitoring the learners' approach to it, the focus is on the outcome. If they produce the right outcome or work to the right standard, it can probably be assumed that they have understood the process that got them there. If they do not, it will be necessary to go back through the process step by step until the point of misunderstanding or the missing skill is identified and rectified.

PLANNING THE FOLLOW-UP

One of the advantages of on-the-job training that we identified in the first section of Chapter 3 was the relative ease with which learning can be transferred back to the job and applied to related tasks. Because the learning is taking place with the regular 'tools of the trade' and in the same context as the work itself, there is no gap between theory and practice. Where off-the-job learning is concerned, this can be a problem.

Take, for example, training someone to conduct a mortgage advice interview. During the training session, a role-play may very well be used to help the learner identify and practise suitable questions to ask the 'mortgage applicant'. If the latter is also a trainee, he or she could be influenced by thoughts like 'It wouldn't be fair to make Shelley look foolish in front of the group – I'll help her out here. It'll be my turn next.'

Even if this sort of contamination does not occur, the context will be different in the real world. There, the applicant may have no idea whether he or she wants a fixed rate, tracker, variable or discounted arrangement, and may be parked on a double yellow line and have lots of shopping and screaming children in tow, whereas the adviser may have a ringing telephone, a deadline to meet for another application and a range of other distractions. How will the trainer, or the learner, be sure that the polished performance observed in the training room will be replicated back at work?

The answer is that neither can. But there is plenty that can be done to increase the chance that it will. In such instances, safeguards include:

- making all examples and practical sessions as realistic as possible. Wherever practicable, 'real' applicants rather then fellow-learners should be used in role-plays of this kind
- debriefing all practical sessions carefully to draw out the similarities, and the differences, between the simulation and the real thing, and to identify strategies for dealing with these
- arranging for the re-entry back at work to be carefully supported by some easily accessible memory-joggers – on cards or captions on the PC, to remind the learner what to do next

■ supervision by an experienced person for the first few real encounters, until the learning has been properly embedded and transfer to other tasks can be seen to be taking place.

Of course none of the above is much use if the training itself is out of touch with current practice. If the pressures at work demand a maximum of five minutes per interview, training that allows 25 will have done little to equip the learner. Yet again we see the importance of being very clear about the objectives to be met and the standards of performance to be achieved. If these have been agreed at the outset, with both the learners and their managers, the transfer back to work will be smoother and the objectives are more likely to be achieved.

SUMMARY: QUICK TIPS

In this chapter we have focused on getting the method and structure right. The following Do's and Don'ts will help to reinforce your learning:

DO:
■ Keep learning objectives constantly in mind.
■ Recognise the preferred learning styles of the learners.
■ Be clear about the resources available and the constraints which apply.
■ Use a range of methods to add variety – but not so many that learners become confused. Think about the sort of mix you have encountered on courses you have been on. What suited you?
■ Familiarise yourself with the particular type of contribution each method can make, and what it will take to use it effectively. The advice in Chapter 6 will help.
■ Make sure the learners' line managers are aware of what can be expected of the learners on their return from training and are ready to provide support to facilitate the transfer of learning back to the workplace and to related tasks.

DON'T:
■ Get carried away with complex designs that lose touch with the reality of what can be achieved during the session or with what will be required back at work.
■ Overlook the fact that learning is what matters. Never select a method because it looks interesting or easy to use. If it is not designed to achieve the kind of learning you need to take place, it will be a waste of time.
■ Forget to build assessment of learners' progress into your design and be thinking about how you will know whether learning has actually taken place (see Chapters 7 and 9).

Materials and facilities

CHAPTER OBJECTIVES

When you have read this chapter you should be able to:

- list at least five different types of learning materials and give an example of a learning objective that would be served by each

- design a flipchart and an overhead projector transparency

- list at least four factors which should be taken into account when selecting training equipment and choosing and using training venues.

CHOOSING LEARNING MATERIALS

The range of possible materials is wide – see Table 17.

Table 17   *Commonly-used learning materials*

Visual aids	Flipcharts, whiteboards (interactive and traditional), overhead projector transparencies (OHTs), Microsoft PowerPoint on-screen slide shows, photographs, models, samples, and dummy material
DVD or video materials	May be used simply to provide illustrative case studies or may introduce an element of interactivity
Workbooks and practice sheets	Either paper-based or electronically delivered online to allow the learner to respond
Training packages	Again either paper-based or electronic and designed either for use by the learner directly or by the trainer to reduce the need for designing from scratch. Training packages may incorporate some or all of the three types of material above, providing workbooks, film clips and photographs, etc
Handouts	Traditional 'chalk and talk' classroom teaching often depended on learners taking copious notes. Sometimes these were dictated aloud or written on a board to be copied. Although the act of writing things down can aid recall, it plays little real role in the learning process unless the learner has to think as well as write. A more efficient use of learning time is for basic facts and key principles to be produced in the form of printed material – perhaps just as copies of Microsoft PowerPoint slides

There are four main factors to consider when deciding what, if any, aids are necessary:

- the needs of the learner

- specific learning objectives
- compatibility with and relevance to other elements of training
- availability.

The needs of the learner

As we saw in Chapter 4, some aids can provide a vehicle for learning in their own right. Workbooks and training packages can allow access to learning at a time and a place and pace to suit the demands of work and domestic life. They can, therefore, provide many of the advantages associated with distance learning that we identified in Chapter 3. If the need is for flexibility, such materials have much to offer. If, on the other hand, the need is for reinforcement of learning as it happens, visual aids used in conjunction with other learning activities and presentations will be helpful. By appealing to more than one sense – eg sight as well as sound – impact and therefore potentially insight and recall will be enhanced.

Specific learning objectives

Much, as always, depends on what the learner needs to be able to do at the end of the session. If the acquisition of a practical skill is the objective, a model or some film footage which enables learners to see what happens when a particular lever is pressed or control activated, can be more helpful than a printed description. Dummy material to practise on may be much more useful than a workbook requiring a description of the steps to take. In first aid training, for example, a life-sized doll whose ribcage can be depressed to practise resuscitation techniques or whose chin can be lifted to clear the airway, can be a better aid than too many diagrams of disconnected internal organs. Where the objective is the development of interpersonal skills, video material showing how not to do it can provide some entertaining insights into the consequences of getting things wrong. It will not be much help in enabling learners to get it right, though, unless alternative positive behaviours (APBs) – ie ways of doing things differently – are identified in follow-up discussion.

Compatibility with and relevance to other elements of training

As we saw in Chapter 4, training should flow logically. The session that is simply a collation of a range of materials that happen to be available is not likely to work. Just as the mix of training methods must be considered, so too must the mix of materials. This can be particularly important when using 'off the shelf' aids. The mix of media, and the mix of messages can be problematic. If bought-in workbooks or other materials are to be used, it is vital to make sure that the information is at the right level and provides the right kind of guidance. A workbook designed for one model of machine or range of products will not necessarily be accurate for a different one. Movie material made some years ago may not just look old-fashioned, it may contain references to obsolete methods or to legislation that has been superseded.

Availability

Most types of learning material can be bought, hired or created in-house. Before planning to use any, make sure that they will be available at the right time. Learning packages online are not normally a problem, but PCs with Internet access might be. Materials that are to be hired must be booked well in advance and checked for compatibility with in-house DVD or video-players. Do not underestimate the time, expertise and cost involved in generating home-made aids. Shooting in-house footage can greatly add to the relevance of some forms of training, including induction, health and safety and customer care. Producing such clips to standards that add value to the training and don't look like the trainer's home movies calls for careful planning and scripting, expert lighting and camera work, extensive editing, and so on. Even a simple OHT or flipchart requires time to prepare properly – see below.

DESIGNING VISUAL AIDS

As should be clear from the previous section, there are some types of aid that demand specialist expertise to produce. Pre-shot movie footage, multimedia and online packages are beyond our present scope, while the range of possible samples and simulation materials is so wide that we can give only a few basic points. These include:

- Make sure that any items used are safe and that you know how to use them.
- Check that they are a close replica of those currently in use in the workplace.
- Make sure that you have enough samples or a big enough replica for all the learners to be able to see, feel, hear, smell or interact as appropriate with it.

Our main focus on this section is on the production of flipcharts, OHTs, Microsoft PowerPoint on-screen slide shows and handout material.

Flipcharts and whiteboards

The use of a flipchart can shape learning and reinforce it. Some trainers prefer to use prepared charts as an alternative to OHTs. Others use them simply to record learners' contributions in class. The advantages and disadvantages of prepared charts are shown in Table 18.

Table 18   *The advantages and disadvantages of prepared flipcharts*

Advantages	Disadvantages
<ul><li>There is no need for specialist equipment – a stretch of empty wall and a piece of BluTack are all you need to display a prepared chart.</li><li>Flipchart pads and pens are relatively cheap and available. They generally cost less per page than OHTs.</li></ul>	<ul><li>That stretch of empty wall may be covered in wallpaper or paint that will be damaged by the BluTack.</li><li>Flipchart paper is difficult to transport without rolling or folding and quickly becomes tatty.</li><li>Each sheet must be displayed separately. There is no scope to build up a series of overlays as there is with OHTs, or, unless folded and pinned very carefully, to disclose the contents a little at a time.</li><li>The lack of magnification demands large, legible, even script which takes time to do well. Even so, learners more than a few metres away may not be able to read it. Errors are hard to erase.</li><li>The fact that the content is normally handwritten limits the possibility for reproducing the content in the form of handouts without re-typing. PowerPoint slides, on the other hand, can be converted to handout format with up to nine slides per page at the click of a mouse button.</li></ul>

The first two of these disadvantages can be overcome by the use of a whiteboard – but this means that the trainer needs time in the training room to write up the content. Almost all the disadvantages can be overcome with an interactive whiteboard – which links to a laptop and allows images to be displayed and amended with a special pen and simple hand movements. The downside of course is the cost, which currently runs into several thousands of pounds.

Overhead transparencies (OHTs) and PowerPoint presentations

These also overcome the disadvantages of the prepared flipchart, but do need more expensive equipment to prepare and present. An overhead projector and screen is needed for OHTs and a laptop, digital projector and screen for a PowerPoint on-screen show. Inexpert use of any medium can significantly detract from the message, so here are a few basic rules to apply when preparing any visual aid.

DO:
- Keep it simple. The more words and figures you use, the less your audience is likely to take in.
- Stick to the point. 'Clip-art' illustrations can distract attention and make slides look too 'busy'.
- Use the visual medium to increase impact and recall – present figures as graphs or charts and substitute relevant pictures for words.
- Use bullet points, not sentences.
- Limit the number of lines per slide – six or eight is the top limit.
- Use as large a font size as you can fit on the slides – 32-point is a good average to aim for.
- Use connectors to help people see the logical flow.
- Check spelling – not just with the spell-check – it won't pick up homophones like 'there' and 'their' if they are correctly spelt .
- Build in the corporate logo or other house-style elements if appropriate.
- Give your audience hard copy after the session to reinforce learning. (If you give them out at the beginning, you will need to keep referring to slide numbers or other identifiers so learners can move at the right pace – although many will choose not to.)
- Control the technology – don't let it control you. Covering an OHT with a sheet of paper and disclosing it gradually is a simple way of helping the audience to focus on each point as you make it. In PowerPoint, the custom animation facility lets you do this electronically.
- Make sure your message is clearly visible – yellows and greens are usually harder to read than black, red or blue. Pale colours will get lost unless you have used a dark background

DON'T:
- Forget the audience. However good your aids are, if you stand in front of them, blocking the view, fail to focus the image, overlap the screen or talk to the aid or the projector instead of to the learners, people will get frustrated and the impact will be lost.
- Become overly reliant on the technology. If a computer or copier failure will mean you are unable to operate, or a spent projector bulb will put you out of action, make sure that if you cannot fix it, you have alternative means of achieving the same learning objectives.
- Get carried away. The interactive whiteboard or PowerPoint presentation may be a powerful tool with lots of functions, but that does not mean you have to use them all to show what a good trainer you are. Bullet points flying every which way may keep the learners awake – but are just as likely to give them a headache. Constant changes of font, size or colour will tend to give away the fact that you are an amateur in the design game.

Handouts

Unless these are to be straight printouts of your slides or transparencies, designed simply as an *aide-mémoire*, you will need to devote as much time to designing them as you do to designing the session – if not more.

DO:
- Be clear about the purpose of the handout – to supplement or reinforce other activities and sources – and state it at the start.
- Structure your ideas logically, as you would for a presentation (see Chapter 6).
- Use graphics and illustrations to enhance understanding.
- Use lots of subheadings and checklists to help the learners find their way through, and to aid revision.
- Keep sentences and paragraphs short and use bullet points or numbers to attract attention.
- Use the corporate house-style if there is one. This could mean a particular font, size, corporate logo, layout or other features. Even if there is no corporate style, adopt a consistent layout within each handout – eg subheadings in bold type, key points listed numerically and subdivided alphabetically. If you are preparing a series of handouts for a longer course, keep the style consistent if you can.

DON'T:
- Re-write the textbook or product manual; keep handouts short and digestible and make sure they 'add value' to other learning methods and materials – and don't just add paper.

CHOOSING EQUIPMENT

Training equipment falls into four broad categories:

- work simulation
- training delivery equipment
- equipment for those with special needs
- specialist equipment for outdoor work.

Work simulation

If you are training someone to drive a forklift truck, a forklift truck would seem to be a useful piece of equipment to have. If you are training someone to operate a checkout terminal, a dummy terminal is invaluable. As with the sample materials mentioned in the previous section, it is inappropriate here to attempt to do more than lay down a few basic guidelines for choosing such equipment. These include:

- Choose either the real thing or as close a copy as possible. This will help the transfer of learning as well as speeding up the learning process by reducing the need for explanations of how the 'real thing' differs.

- Make sure the equipment is safe to operate, bearing in mind the present skill level of the learners. Dual controls, emergency overrides, dummy data, training data sets and parallel systems are among the safeguards which may prevent accidents or injury or the loss or corruption of important data.

- Remember that equipment alone does not enable learning. The learner will need something or someone to assist movement around the learning cycle. That could be a coach constantly probing to get the learner to 'Think what will happen if you press this/turn that/do this' before each action and/or to check 'What did you notice?', 'What effect did that have?', 'What difference did that make?' to raise awareness afterwards. A workbook, CD-ROM or online program which asks the same questions can serve the same purpose.

Training delivery equipment

We have already mentioned the most frequently-used items of training equipment. These include:

- flipcharts and stands
- overhead projectors (OHPs) and screens
- whiteboards and interactive whiteboards
- laptops and digital projectors
- video/digital cameras/webcams and associated playback facilities.

Your choice will be influenced by :

- the needs of the learner. The fact that the training department has just acquired a sophisticated webcam does not mean that every minute of every training session must be recorded for posterity. Unless speed, flexibility and instant playback facilities will enhance learning, it will be a distraction. Where learners are grappling with complex physical tasks and will benefit from seeing their actions and their effects in close detail, though, such equipment is invaluable in helping them to see for themselves what is happening. Whether a webcam or an old-fashioned video camera is appropriate will depend on the resources of the training department and the expertise of the trainer. Either piece of equipment will be ineffective in the hands of a trainer who has not mastered the 'on/off' switch, the lens cap or the 'record' button
- learning objectives. If the objective is the development of skills, a recording which enhances the learners' awareness of their own actions will help. If the objective is to provide an understanding of underpinning concepts, a visual aid or a handout to state and reinforce these will be of more value
- availability of compatible equipment. A camcorder is not much use without the facilities to play back the sound and images recorded. A flipchart pad is difficult to use effectively without a stand. A laptop with no digital projector will be of limited use if there are more than a couple of learners
- availability of expertise. In the hands of a skilled trainer a simple flipchart used to draw ideas together and link them to the learning objective is of more value than an interactive whiteboard in the hands of a novice untrained in its use
- reliability. This is possibly the most critical factor to consider when choosing training equipment. Equipment which refuses to function can be worse than no equipment at all. As a basic rule, the more complex the equipment is to set up and use, the more the chance that the previous user has left it unusable. A neatly folding OHP is a very valuable aid for the trainer on the move – but not if the instructions for dismantling it are so complicated that key components get broken in the process. In view of the wear and tear that some equipment receives, reliability is a key issue – not just in the choice of the supplier and the model, but in terms of the type of equipment itself
- functionality. Some equipment can be used for more than one purpose. The purchase of a PC may, for example, allow among other things:
  - training records to be kept (see Chapter 10)
  - PowerPoint presentations to be made
  - a webcam to be used
  - Internet and online learning packages to be accessed by learners directly or by trainers for source materials
  - online assessment of learners' progress (Chapter 7)
  - online evaluation of training with quick and easy analysis of results – see Chapter 9.

Even quite simple equipment can open up a more varied set of training options. The purchase of an OHP will mean that learners can be asked to produce transparencies too. These are often easier for the novice to handle than the flipchart alternative and give the trainer a permanent record of, for example, group discussions. This can be taken away, copied and returned to the learners as a handout without the need for expensive retyping.

■ cost. It is not just the capital outlay and associated depreciation that may have to be considered. The cost of the 'consumables' the equipment uses must also be borne in mind. Replacement ink or toner cartridges, bulbs, special pens or markers, acetates for use with different types of printer – each comes at a price which can make inroads into a tight training budget.

Equipment for those with special needs

The types of equipment so far discussed tend to be for use primarily by the trainer. For some learners, though, additional equipment may be needed so that they are not at a disadvantage. For the visually impaired, special computer programs are available to enable them to 'see' material. For the hearing impaired, hearing loops can be installed to help them follow the trainer's input. Adapted seating or working arrangements may be needed to enable someone with reduced physical mobility to take part fully in the training he or she needs to do the job. As we saw in Chapter 1, the Disability Discrimination Act makes it imperative for employers to make reasonable adjustments – and that means in the training room too. Special grants may be available to help with the cost, and it is worth contacting the local Jobcentre Plus to find out.

Specialist equipment for outdoor work

Some types of training call for equipment which does not fit into any of the above categories. Outdoor training, often used to help develop teamworking and leadership skills, has its own particular requirements. These can range from tents and sleeping-bags to accommodate learners, through to an assortment of ladders, ropes, beams, buckets and other items to be used as obstacles or challenges. As with all other types of equipment, health and safety and fitness for purpose are the paramount considerations.

CHOOSING VENUES

Some types of training can be conducted almost anywhere. Others need an array of specialist facilities. In Chapter 3 the advantages of on- and off-the-job training were examined and the range of possible external providers was discussed. The choice of learning venue will, in many cases, be determined by the outcome of those two sets of decisions. Where learning is to be off-the-job but not at a venue prescribed by the choice of provider, the key decision is whether to remain 'on-site' – ie on your employer's premises – or to take the training off-site.

If there is no dedicated space available at the workplace, the question does not arise. If there is, the advantages and disadvantages of each option have to be considered.

On-site training has the advantages of

■ accessibility for learners and trainers
■ familiarity for learners and trainers
■ lower cost
■ (probably) easier access to back-up for trainers – to fix equipment, provide specialist input or a visit to a workshop or office to test something out in practice
■ less anxiety for learners suffering withdrawal symptoms from their desks or workstations
■ the feeling that this is 'just another day at the office', enhancing the belief that learning is a normal part of working.

The disadvantages are:

- possible distractions. The temptation for delegates to call in to check their e-mail or the post on the way in or at lunchtime, or the boss who 'only needs him or her for a minute' are just some of the potential hazards
- the space provided may not really be suitable for the type of learning required. So-called 'training rooms' often have to double as meeting rooms, store rooms or even sick rooms or prayer rooms, leading to extraneous equipment being stored there and less flexibility of seating and layout. Even in quite large organisations, the availability of 'break-out rooms' for group work and social space for refreshments can be limited. In many small ones, such facilities are non-existent
- catering may not be available without going off-site or visiting the canteen – increasing the risk of distractions
- there may not be anyone to help set up and manage the location, increasing the risk of distractions for the trainer
- the feeling that 'this is just another day at the office' can have an adverse impact on motivation to learn.

The feasibility of taking training off-site to counter these disadvantages will depend on

- budget
- the availability of appropriate venues
- the ease with which any necessary equipment or staff can be transported to the venue
- the length of the training session. Unless the alternative venue is very close, it may not be worth going off-site for just an hour or two. The disruption to the working day may be too great.

Wherever the training is to take place, the room should be

- light and airy
- quiet and free from distractions (including telephones)
- equipped with flexible, easily moved furniture to allow a range of possible layouts, from a simple semicircle of chairs, through 'cabaret style' where sets of four to six people can sit round tables, to more formal 'horse-shoes' of tables and chairs
- furnished with screen, whiteboard, flipchart(s), overhead projector and (for role-play and some practical exercises) cameras and playback facilities, plus the necessary power sources and black-out arrangements/curtains to prevent sunlight obliterating the view
- provided with BluTack-friendly walls or plenty of board space to pin up flipchart paper
- big enough to accommodate the whole learning group, and supported by separate syndicate/break-out rooms if necessary.

SETTING UP THE LOCATION

Many adult learners have negative recollections of their schooldays. Whatever the learning objectives, the connotations of the conventional classroom will often be counter-productive. In setting out the room, make sure you consider the methods you are planning to use and the possible barriers to learning discussed in the first section of Chapter 6. Bear in mind:

- The need for visual contact. If there is to be interaction between learners – discussions, or a case study perhaps – make sure that learners can see each other as well as the trainer. Consider whether name-plates or badges would help those who have not met before. Blank cards for the learners to complete are a quick and inexpensive way of making sure delegates are referred to by their preferred names, rather than what it says on their personnel record. Pre-printed labels do look more professional, though, so the choice will depend on the level of formality you wish to create.

- Audibility. If the session is to be at all participative, learners will make contributions 'from the floor'. How will you ensure that everyone can hear each other? Layout can help, but in a large room with lots of delegates, a roving microphone will be needed.

- The visibility of visual aids. Check that the screen, whiteboard and flipchart can be clearly seen from all parts of the room and that you can position yourself somewhere where you will not block anyone's view, where you will be comfortable to stand or sit, and will have ready access to the aids you plan to use.

- The accessibility of materials. Make sure that any written briefs, handouts, task sheets, workbooks, etc are set out where you can lay your hands on them quickly and easily at the right moment.

- Health, safety and learner welfare.
  - Check that the room is clean and smells fresh. There are few things more off-putting for trainees than having to work in a hot, stale atmosphere. At best they will find it soporific.
  - Similarly, make sure that any debris from previous sessions is cleared away. Pens, paper, coffee cups, plates, etc should be removed when no longer in use.
  - If learners are expected to make notes, provide them with pads and pencils. If they are to be given handouts and other written material, a ring binder each and a hole punch can be added.
  - Check the temperature of the room at intervals during the session. If learners are sitting still listening to presentations, they will have a lot less adrenaline to keep them warm than the speaker will. Do not wait for people to start putting on their coats before turning up the thermostat.
  - Check the room for hazards like trailing cables before you start. These can be covered with a rubber strip or taped down to avoid trips and falls. Badly-fitting windows and doors, wobbly furniture, fixtures and fittings constitute further hazards, as do any items left lying around for people, particularly the visually impaired, to trip over.
  - Familiarise yourself with fire evacuation procedures and what to do in the event of an emergency so you can brief the learners properly when they arrive.

- Barriers to learning. We will explore these in more detail in Chapter 6. Here it is sufficient to note that the room should be configured to keep external distractions to a minimum. Position learners with their backs to the windows or other likely sources of distraction. If there is a telephone in the room, consider disconnecting it. Check whether there are any noisy activities such as building work or grass-cutting scheduled to take place while the session is in progress.

SUMMARY: QUICK TIPS

In this chapter we have focused on the key decisions you will need to make about materials, equipment and the training venue. To reinforce your learning:

DO:

- Be guided throughout by the needs of the learners and the particular objectives of the session.
- Put yourself in the learners' shoes. Will these materials help them to understand better or get more skilled more quickly? Only if the answer is 'yes' are they likely to be worth using.
- Keep the practicalities firmly in view. Fancy materials which distract people, or equipment which is unreliable or which you are not confident and competent in using, are best avoided.
- Remember you must work to a training budget (Chapter 10). Use the equipment you have rather than building up an expensive wish-list that is unlikely ever to get capital expenditure approval.
- Put health and safety at the top of your list in choosing and using equipment and venues, and pay particular attention to the needs of those with disabilities.

DON'T:

- Be seduced into using materials, equipment or venues because they 'look good'. If they are not fit for the purpose or if they fail to add value to the achievement of learning objectives, they are at best a waste of money and at worst will detract from learning.

Delivering training

IDENTIFYING BARRIERS TO LEARNING

Very young children learn naturally. Curiosity – the need to find out what, how, why – is a very positive stimulus to learning. As we get older, other factors may come into play to make it more difficult to learn. Some of these are internal to the individual, some relate to the environment in which learning is intended to take place, or to the trainer or the other learners involved.

Internal barriers

These take four main forms, which may operate separately or be interconnected:

- negative previous experience
- negative aptitude
- negative prior attainment
- negative motivation.

Negative previous experience

People whose experience of learning at school was poor may tend to expect that all learning will be as boring/irrelevant/uncomfortable/difficult as their schooldays. These expectations will influence how receptive they are to the very idea of further formal learning and will influence their willingness to learn and their mindset during training.

Negative aptitude

Someone with poor physical co-ordination is likely to find it harder to get to grips with psychomotor tasks that require manipulative dexterity. A person with poor short-term memory will find it harder to remember the key steps in a process or important facts. The level and speed of cognitive ability (thinking skills) will influence whether and how quickly each individual grasps new concepts and ways of working.

Negative prior attainment

Learners who have missed out on the basics of the subject may well find this an obstacle to further learning. Lack of essential literacy, numeracy or IT skills can be a particular barrier, not least because people sometimes go to great lengths to conceal the fact that they cannot read or write.

Negative motivation

The Otto and Glaser model described in Chapter 1 (*What makes training work?*) provides a framework for understanding the motivational forces which can influence people's approach to and willingness to learn. Fear of failure can be a particular issue for adult learners, perhaps linking back to previous negative experience at school. Table 19 sets out some brief pointers to ways in which these internal barriers may be countered or overcome.

CASE STUDY

Finding the level

A major construction company was keen to up-skill its workforce and asked a local college to introduce an NVQ programme for potential site supervisors. Twelve months on, only three of the 12 learners were still persevering with the programme. The trainer talked to each of those who had dropped out and eventually discovered that six of them had given up because they found it too difficult and were struggling to read the course materials. For the next round of the programme, all course documents were revised to make sure that they did not demand an inappropriately high level of language proficiency. Prospective learners were invited to undertake a diagnostic test to assess which NVQ level they should be working towards. Some then started work at level 2 and some at level 3, while all who needed it were given support in reading skills, writing, or numeracy, as appropriate. This time, of eight starters, all but one successfully completed the programme. By finding out where the learners were starting from, the problem was solved.

Are there any courses running in your organisation which may not have been pitched at the right level or where learners could benefit from some additional support?

Environmental barriers

The environment can play a positive role in stimulating curiosity, or a negative one in reminding learners of unsuccessful school experiences. Environmental barriers go beyond this to include anything that adversely affects concentration, motivation or progress around the learning cycle. Failure to pay attention to any of the health, safety and welfare aspects detailed in Chapter 5 will tend to build up such barriers, and in particular:

- Extremes of temperature or noise or a stuffy atmosphere will make it hard to concentrate.
- Lighting that is too bright or too dark will impair visibility.
- Telephone calls and other interruptions will break the flow and remind learners of the outside world.
- Equipment breakdowns may prevent or reduce the learning that can take place.

Other learners

Wherever a group comes together to learn, the range of learning styles, personalities and individual motivation can create barriers to each other's learning. The only theorist in a group of activists may find that

Table 19   *Internal barriers to learning*

Barrier	Possible remedy
Negative previous experience	Look for ways of signalling that it will be different this time. Avoid 'classroom' layouts and environments, take the learning to the learner, use on-the-job or familiar surroundings that do not look or feel like school; avoid 'chalk and talk' and unconstructive feedback to learners.
Negative aptitude	If learners are having difficulty coping with training, discuss this with HR colleagues. It may be that some prior testing to establish the level of aptitude could establish whether new recruits have the potential to acquire particular skills. Proprietary tests of manipulative dexterity, hand-eye co-ordination, critical thinking, spatial awareness, etc are available but must be administered by a qualified administrator. Alternatively, the use of a specially designed 'trainability test' could be considered as part of the selection process. This would involve training potential recruits on a key task and then assessing their performance. Only those who demonstrate that they are 'trainable' should be selected. Within the training session, if someone is struggling to grasp a particular concept or manoeuvre, establish his or her preferred learning style and use it to help him or her overcome the stumbling-block.
Negative attainment	The best principle is to 'start from where the learner is'. Pay attention to the *prior* sequence in which component elements are taught, to make sure that you are not asking learners to run before they can walk. Pay particular attention to anyone who starts the course late – it can sometimes be counter-productive, for him or her and for other learners, to let him or her take part if too much has been missed already. The case study above addresses the essential skills issue.
Negative motivation	To counteract fear of failure, design the training to provide some 'quick wins' – to provide early experience of success. 'Chunking' the learning up into small steps so that it does not appear too daunting may also help. Make sure that learners get positive feedback to increase their feeling of self-worth and approval. Build in avenues for the curious to explore, and encourage a sense of achievement by helping learners to set their own goals and monitor progress towards them. Knowledge of results is key to sustaining motivation. This can be external – in the form of feedback from the trainer or other learners – or internal – the learner can tell that he or she has done it right because he or she has been able to progress to the next step. Some e-learning operates in this way. The more self-sufficient learners become, and the less dependent on the trainer for feedback and approbation, the more likely they are to take responsibility for their own learning – see *Creating the right climate* later in this chapter.

training becomes too action-packed. The person who is anxious above all to avoid failure may find it hard to learn alongside people motivated by the need to achieve. If they are working on tasks together, their different natural approaches can give rise to tensions with which they may not know how to deal. Add to this a mixture of status, cultures, values and behaviour, and some learners may spend more time thinking about the 'chauvinist from sales' or 'that fascist/reactionary/lefty from accounts' than they do about the learning itself. The art of the trainer lies in encouraging inclusivity (see *Ensuring inclusivity* below) by bringing together people from different backgrounds, while not allowing their differences to get in the way of learning. A good mix in every group is ideal, with a watchful eye to see that no one is feeling left out. To understand how groups work together, the analysis of group dynamics (the penultimate section of this chapter) can help.

The trainer

Quite apart from failure to recognise or deal with other barriers to learning, it is all too easy for trainers to behave in a way that antagonises or distracts learners, thereby creating a further barrier. In Chapter 11 we highlight the range of skills that trainers need, but sensitivity to the impact their behaviour has on others is high on the list. Trainer-created barriers include:

- constant use of particular words or phrases – this can mean that learners spend more time waiting for the next 'actually' or 'you see' than they do attending to content
- distracting mannerisms, like strumming fingers or fiddling with pens, which can have a similar effect
- drawing examples from too limited a range, which can leave learners from a different background or part of the organisation feeling left out
- focusing on particular individuals, directing questions to or engaging in dialogue with the same people all the time, which risks others 'switching off'
- making inappropriate or risqué remarks based on race or gender, which will alienate some learners
- appearing not to listen to or be concerned about the welfare or progress of learners, which will also have a negative effect – as may too much praise or insincerity.

Careful planning is one means of reducing the likelihood that you will create any of these barriers. Continuous monitoring of learner reactions is the other key to avoiding the pitfalls. Pay attention to all the members of the group and watch for signs that they are switching off or becoming confused or negative. Some will make this obvious, fidgeting, looking out of the window, doodling or refusing to get involved. Others may be harder to spot.

CREATING THE RIGHT CLIMATE

Part of this is about avoiding the barriers identified in the previous section and part of it is about the selection of venues and materials outlined in Chapter 5. But more than this, creating a climate conducive to learning is about making the right assumptions. An understanding of the learning cycle and theories of learning is part of the story, but there is something more subtle than this that goes to the heart of the trainers' value system and beliefs about people.

In *Coaching for Performance* John Whitmore identifies two qualities that are crucial to performance in any activity. These are *awareness* and *responsibility*.

Awareness

The learner who blindly follows the directions of the trainer is not actually learning at all. At best such 'learners' may be able to recall the steps taken and repeat them until they become a habit. But for understanding, application and transfer, awareness is essential. Unless learners are conscious of their own actions and their consequences, movement around the learning cycle is impaired. 'When I do this, that happens' is the basis of theorising. Without it, people cannot see the connections between their actions and the results, and will not be able to generalise from one situation to another. With it, even low levels of skill can be enhanced.

Responsibility

Responsibility is the opposite of dependency. The responsible learner takes the initiative rather than expecting to be told what to do. When people take it upon themselves to find out – because they want to – issues associated with lack of motivation just evaporate. Telling learners what to do denies them the chance to take responsibility themselves. Constantly telling them how they are doing and praising them for their efforts will provide positive reinforcement – but may also deny them the chance to become more responsible and self-aware.

When self-aware learners take responsibility for their own learning, performance can improve beyond all recognition – not because of the skill of the trainer but because the talent latent within the individual has been allowed to flourish. So how do you, the trainer, create the sort of climate where this happens?

The key lies in the mindset with which you approach the task of training. If you seek to be the source of all wisdom, expecting learners to hang on your every word, you are likely to find that the sort of barriers described in the previous section easily block learning. If you put the learners first, and embrace the belief that each is capable of much more than at present seems possible, you are on the right road. The higher your expectations, the more likely it is that people will exceed them. That is the philosophy which is most likely to lead to real learning and high performance.

ENSURING INCLUSIVITY

In Chapter 1 we explored the legal framework within which the trainer must operate and noted the definitions of direct and indirect discrimination. The key to this, and to ensuring inclusivity, is not to make assumptions about people based on who they are, where they come from, or their physical or mental condition. Focusing on each learner as an individual with untapped potential, rather than as a member of a particular part of society, you won't go far wrong.

COACHING, QUESTIONING AND LISTENING

From our discussion so far it will be clear that these three skills are fundamental for the trainer.

Coaching

The GROW model outlined in Chapter 4 (in a subsection also entitled *Coaching*) provides a framework for coaching which is consistent with a training philosophy based on awareness-raising and responsibility. Whatever an employee needs to learn, being clear about the specific goals and the present position in relation to them must be the starting point. Encouraging experimentation and reflection, rather than simply 'telling', will enhance ownership and a sense of responsibility for learning. Enquiring 'What do you notice?', 'What do you feel?', 'What is happening now?' while the learner is trying something new, may be all that is needed to help focus, raise awareness, and promote learning.

Because coaching is based on 'asking' rather than 'telling', being an effective coach requires both effective questioning and effective listening skills.

Questioning techniques

As we saw in Chapter 4, there are two main types of question and a number of variations. By using each appropriately you can open up and close down the flow of information and help learners focus on what is important.

Open questions
These invite more than a one-word answer. They usually start with

- 'What . . .?'   eg 'What else do you notice?'
- 'How . . .?'   eg 'How did that feel to you?'
- 'Why . . .?'   eg 'Why do you think that happened?'

The same effect can be achieved by phrases used as questions, such as

- 'I wonder if you can think of an example of . . . ?'
- 'It might be useful to recall . . . '

or by direct requests like

- 'Would you enlarge on that a little, please?'

For the taciturn learner, or to get a range of issues and ideas, the open question is often a good starting point.

Closed or direct questions
These invite only a one-word or very brief answer. They often start with

- 'When . . . ?'   eg 'When was that?'
- 'Where . . . ?'   eg 'Where were you when it happened?'
- 'Who . . . ?'   eg 'Who else was involved?'
- 'How many . . . ?'   eg 'How many times did you do that?'

The replies are likely to be explicit and factual. Closed questions are particularly helpful to encourage learners to focus on what is actually happening. Too many of them in rapid succession can begin to feel like a bit of an inquisition, though, and will not open up debate.

Leading or rhetorical questions
These are phrased to anticipate the correct response, as in

- 'You do agree, don't you?'

or

- 'We wouldn't want to do that, would we?'

The first presumes the answer 'yes', the second 'no'. Both are best avoided. They do not oblige the learners to think. They can also easily sound patronising.

Multiple questions
In trying to make your questions clear and easy to understand, you may find yourself amplifying what started off as a simply-worded question. When this happens, you will probably end up with a multiple question. For instance:

- 'Did any of you notice what happened when Sol asked Mary how she felt? Was his timing right, or should he not have interrupted her – what could you tell from her body language? I mean, was there anything in particular evident at the time?'

The learners are faced with a choice of questions and will not know whether to focus on timing, body language, or something else entirely.

Probing/follow-up questions
Whatever type of question you have asked, never be frightened to probe a little further:

- 'What else?'
- 'What then?'
- 'What more?'

Such questions help to check understanding, challenge further thought, and/or sharpen the focus.

Listening

Often you will be aware that you are only half-listening. The car radio does (or should) not claim your full attention when you are driving. Many people read the newspaper, cook or do the ironing while apparently listening to the radio or watching TV. The quality of listening on such occasions is unlikely to be at the level you need to help learners progress around the learning cycle. For that, you need real concentration and awareness. To help:

- Make sure that the choice and setup of the training room is conducive to concentration (see *Internal barriers* above).
- Get organised so that you can give the learners your undivided attention. The pile of correspondence on your desk, the appointment you forgot this morning, the telephone call you need to make before lunch, and a thousand and one other things will all distract you if you cannot manage your time (see Chapter 11).
- Make sure that you are as fresh and alert as possible. Tiredness, ill health or even an uncomfortable sitting position can cause your mind to wander instead of listening to what learners are saying.
- Use linking questions and regular summaries to force yourself to listen. If you know you will need to start each question by a reference back to a previous answer, it really concentrates the mind. So if one learner has said

    'Well, I think the wind speed may have a bearing . . .',

    your next question would start

    'Josh has mentioned the impact of wind speed – now, what else ought to be taken into account?'
- Above all, stay interested. If you genuinely want to help your learners to learn and believe that they have the potential to achieve, you will find it much easier to pay attention at the right level. If you would rather be somewhere else, with a brighter group of learners, you are unlikely to listen effectively.

MAKING A PRESENTATION

The effectiveness of a lecture or presentation depends on the clarity of its objectives and the extent to which the audience buy into them. If the presenter's aim is to win an Oscar and the audience are there to find out about the subject, the two may not be compatible.

- Tell them what you're going to tell them.
- Tell them.
- Tell them you've told them.

Structuring a presentation around these principles may be a rather traditional approach – but it works. It means you will need to:

- Explain the structure of your presentation at the start.
- Present the content in a way that captures the attention and imagination of your audience.

- Summarise the key points at the end to make sure that the learners go away with the right message.

Unless your presentation is to be very short – and most people's attention span is less than 20 minutes – you may need to use other media to help (see Chapter 5). Below are some further pointers to assist you.

Tips for effective presentations

- Structure your material – by building a framework to help people remember. Some subjects lend themselves to a chronological approach, others may follow a 'who, what, why, how, when, where' sequence. Sometimes it will be necessary to work through the material several times during your preparation, putting key points on 'Post-Its' which can be clustered and re-clustered until a framework emerges that you can use.
- Decide your policy on questions. Will you ask some questions of the audience at the beginning, to check where they are starting from – in the middle, to check that they are awake and you are on the right track – at the end, to check their understanding – or all three? Do you want to invite questions from them during the presentation or only at the end?
- Share your plans – the objectives of the presentation and the route you plan to take to achieve them do not need to be a closely guarded secret. Let the audience know what to expect.
- Build in signposts to help the audience follow your structure and remember it. As well as outlining it at the beginning, draw attention to where you have got to from time to time. Visual aids can help, and so can regular summaries.
- Rehearse to make sure you know how long your presentation takes. You need to experience how it sounds when spoken out loud. Ideally, get feedback from a guinea-pig to help you identify points that need clarification and to advise on pace and impact.
- Check your timing – and have a contingency plan in case questions take more or less time than you anticipate.

Making a good presentation takes practice and patience and, above all, meticulous planning. It also requires the ability to think on your feet. If your questions highlight that your audience are on a different wavelength, you will have to decide whether to plod on anyway or try to tailor your presentation accordingly. If their questions to you seem to be going back over old ground, you will have to decide whether to repeat the key points, try to re-state them in a different way, ask another member of the group if he or she can summarise the issue, or tell the questioner off for not listening.

If your audience challenges the view that you have been putting forward, you will have to decide whether to leap to your own defence, enter into a debate, or try to understand the questioners' perspective. When you have spent hours preparing what you thought was the definitive last word on the subject, it can be disconcerting when someone appears to disagree. You must be able to de-personalise the issue and see all questions as expressions of interest rather than as challenges or threats. The checklist below highlights some of the things you should try to cultivate that should help you make effective presentations.

Checklist of characteristics of effective presenters

- a clear and pleasant speaking voice, which conveys enthusiasm for the subject without sounding over the top – sincerity without apparent superficiality – and which rises and falls naturally to retain interest
- no distracting verbal mannerisms

- no distracting physical mannerisms – controlling any such mannerism, perhaps by putting one hand firmly in your pocket at the start of the session, is important
- personal 'presence', to draw the attention of your audience and make them want to listen – if you are too timid or uncertain, they will not take you seriously; if you are too dogmatic or pushy, they may react negatively
- empathy with and interest in your audience – if you don't care whether or not they listen and learn, they may not either. Make sure you look at them while you are speaking – maintaining eye contact with each member of the audience draws them in to your presentation
- effective questioning skills, to ask questions of your audience as an aid to establishing empathy and rapport, checking how best to make your material really relevant, and testing reactions and understanding (see section above)

ROLE-PLAYS

This method requires one or more of the learners to assume a role other than his or her own. A good deal of sales training, for instance, includes the role-playing of customers. Some safety-awareness training puts learners in the role of supervisor or safety trainer. Some interview skills training puts trainees in the role of candidate, aggrieved employee or appraisee.

What all have in common is their overall objective. By asking someone to play a role other than his or her own, it is possible to help him or her see the world through a different perspective. The 'safety supervisor' required to persuade a colleague to wear personal protective equipment may, in the process of marshalling the arguments, convince himself or herself. The 'customer who has been shabbily treated by the company' may begin to understand some of the tensions and anxieties customers feel when they come to complain.

At the same time, the other participant(s) in the role-play should develop their competence in dealing with such situations. The sales person learns how to deal with an irate customer. The manager learns to conduct an effective interview. Many learners find that role-plays provide invaluable interpersonal and attitude skills training.

Some, though, find role-playing quite stressful. Others may dismiss it as 'play-acting' with no relevance to real life. Managing a successful session requires careful selection of material, ample briefing and skilled debriefing to help participants confront their learning without damaging their self-esteem.

Wherever possible, real-life examples should be used. It helps, too, if the person whose skills you are trying to develop is able, so far as possible, to be themselves – acting as they think appropriate to the situation – rather than taking on the personality of some fictitious character.

If you are writing role-plays,

DO:
- Make sure you have a clear understanding of the learning objectives to be achieved or the competencies to be developed.
- Think up scenarios which are realistic and relevant.
- Prepare briefing and debriefing materials thoroughly. Keep them as simple as possible to allow participants scope to be themselves as far as possible.
- Be consistent – you may not give all the characters the same information, but it should all hang together when the full story emerges.

> **DON'T:**
> ■ Make briefs so complex that participants are more worried about remembering the details than about executing the role.

As with any other form of practical exercise, it is not the five minutes or the 35 minutes of the role-play which are key. It is the preparation and follow-up that matter most. You should:

■ Plan the time allocation carefully. If several learners are involved, all must have time to give and receive feedback.

■ Manage the feedback constructively – see *Giving feedback* below. It is usually best to ask the key player, the person whose skills you have been trying to develop, to talk through how it felt and what did and did not go according to plan before inviting any of the other participants to contribute or giving feedback yourself. Everyone should be encouraged to reflect back what they saw happening and to comment on the observed effects of this – rather than indulge in personal emotions, praise or blame. If the trainee is not yet 100-per-cent competent, the quest must be for alternative positive behaviour – what could he or she have done instead?

■ Consider preparing structured report forms, for all participants and observers. These will help to create the right tone if they focus on what was actually said or done and its observed effects, rather than on personalities or emotions.

GROUP DISCUSSIONS

Any group coming together for the first time goes through the four phases shown in Table 20. Only if they work together through all four stages can they truly be said to have become a 'team'.

Table 20 *Stages in team development*

Stage	Description
Forming	People come together for the first time and size each other up. This is a phase of tentative exploration and a desire to gain acceptance – to belong to the group.
Storming	Once people know each other a little better, the power-play starts. A pecking-order gets established, and the leadership of the group may change hands.
Norming	At this point, members have come to terms with each other's strengths and weaknesses and recognise the role each can play.
Performing	This is when the whole team is working co-operatively together to achieve the common goal, each person making his or her own best contribution to success.

It can take months or even years, with careful coaching or expert leadership to get through all four stages. Throwing people together in groups and expecting them to 'perform' in a training context is therefore a forlorn hope. In the short term this may not matter too much if you can keep all group members focused on the task the group has been set. But if you want groups to work together over a long period, you may need to start by raising awareness of the characteristics of effective teams and doing some analysis of team roles – see Table 21.

To conduct an effective group discussion session:

DO:

- Make sure learners know what the learning objective is. This will help them get the right balance between discussion of the topic and presentation of their conclusions. If the presentation is to senior management and may form part of the evaluation of the training (see Chapter 9), it will need a lot more attention to form and style than if it is simply a quick sharing of ideas with other groups.
- Specify clearly the brief to which the group should work and the outcome(s) they should produce. This could be a list of options or action points or a full action plan, an agreed statement, a list of factors to consider or of situations in which particular approaches can be applied. If the brief is at all complex, it will be useful to issue it in writing for groups to refer back to.
- Be clear who is to lead or chair the discussion and who is to act as scribe or secretary. Someone nominated by the group or by the trainer can fill these roles. The proficiency of those chosen can have an impact on how group members feel about the outcome of their deliberations. Will the chair or someone else be required to report the group's findings in plenary session? Some otherwise very capable people may find this quite daunting. If the topic is an important one and/or the group is to stay in being for some time, encourage them to think hard about what each role requires and who can best fill it
- Let learners know how long they have for the discussion and what they will be expected to do at the end: a presentation to other groups in plenary session, a written report or an individual write-up. How long should presentations last? What form should they take? What aids do they have – flipchart, OHP, interactive whiteboards, etc.
- Make sure that learners have the information they need to make the discussion meaningful or that they can readily get access to it.
- Pay careful attention to the composition of the groups. Depending on the learning objective, learning styles and mix of experience and personalities involved, you may want to aim for a mix of types within each group and a fair spread of expertise between groups. If the discussion group is to be a long-term feature of the training – perhaps as part of an action learning programme in which training is interspersed with periods back at work – it may be worth doing some formal role analysis to make sure that there is a good mix of the approaches listed in Table 21 below.
- Monitor progress regularly. However clear the initial objective and brief were, once the discussion gets going, learners may follow their own interests and lose the plot.
- Make sure that groups have the resources they need – flipchart paper, acetates/OHPs, etc; give regular time-checks.
- Determine your policy on teams getting together to compare notes/exchange ideas ahead of the plenary session. Whether this matters will depend on the learning objectives. Similarly, think about how you will react if asked to give additional information to one or more of the groups.

DON'T:

- Join in to steer the debate. If necessary, get groups back on track through a few carefully chosen questions about how their ideas relate to the brief they have been given.
- Obviously eavesdrop – you could deflect the group from the task without adding any value.
- Be surprised if groups come back with answers to what looks like a different question from the one you thought you had asked. Unless the brief is very tight, your monitoring frequent and the range of options very limited, some natural variation is inevitable. If this invalidates the learning objective, it means that either the brief was unclear or your monitoring has been insufficient.
- Underestimate how long most discussions take – particularly if the group is working together for the first time. You may need to progress-chase to make sure they allow enough time to prepare their presentation.

Table 21 *Team roles (based on work by Dr Meredith Belbin)*

Role	Contribution
'Plant'	ideas
Resource investigator	information and resources
'Shaper'	clarification of objectives
Monitor/evaluator	analysis
Specialist	focus on the task
Implementer	practical common sense
Teamworker	support for colleagues
'Completer'	checking for loose ends
Co-ordinator	drawing contributions together

GROUP EXERCISES

Many of the principles identified for conducting group discussions will also apply in other forms of group work. Group exercises put real trainees in real or simulated situations. They take many forms. From practice sessions on workplace machinery to interactive media-based activity, from business simulations to outdoor leadership and team-building tasks. The range is huge. At a general level the objective will be similar – that is, to provide an opportunity for the learners to learn through experience rather than on the basis of abstract theory alone.

Herein lies the key to the effective use of such exercises. Experience alone may teach us very little. It is reflection on that experience and the chance to work out alternative ways of tackling it before trying again that really moves people around the learning cycle. Whether it is designed to help a trainee accountant to construct a budget or a trainee manager to lead a team in a crisis, the exercise itself can only be part of the learning experience.

With this in mind, practical exercises should be approached as a means to an end rather than an end in themselves. Beware the trainer who sets the learner(s) up with an exercise and then goes off to do something else while they get on with it. It may not be necessary for the trainer to breathe down learners' necks all the time, but he or she almost certainly needs to be available to:

- clarify the task and the objectives
- advise on resources to help
- observe any points of confusion not deliberately built into the exercise
- ensure the safety of the trainee(s), especially in the case of outdoor and machine-based exercises
- coach and debrief after the event to help the trainee(s) reflect and draw out key learning.

Do not be misled into thinking that setting exercises is the easy way of training. Physically, mentally and emotionally it can be quite demanding. There is a real danger in focusing on the exercises themselves rather than on the learning they are designed to achieve. If you are involved in designing exercises of any sort you will need to:

- be fully conversant with the learning objectives
- understand the competencies to be developed
- have the imagination to create situations or scenarios in which such competencies can be tested or developed
- have the attention to detail to make sure that there are no accidental inconsistencies in the information given to participants.

GROUP DYNAMICS

Some of the characteristics associated with group behaviour and team membership were highlighted in *Group discussions* above. These provide a good starting point for understanding how members of a group may interact with each other – ie the dynamic they will create. How this translates into actual behaviour will be influenced by whether or not learners knew each other before attending the training and, if they work for the same organisation, their relative positions within it. Having the managing director as a participant will, in most organisations, affect the behaviour of more junior employees. Some may seek to shine and become much more vocal. Others may try to hide and be harder to get involved. This is an extreme example, perhaps, but external factors like this really do make a difference to how learners function as a group.

The best recipe for managing these issues and for making sure that everyone works together to increase the chances of achieving the learning objectives is to:

- be as aware as possible of the factors likely to influence the behaviour of individuals and the group
- make sure that learners are aware of the effect their own behaviour has on others.

Whenever a group of learners comes together for the first time, it is a good idea to 'break the ice' by the use of a few non-threatening 'get to know you' techniques.

- Ask participants to work in pairs to interview each other for about three minutes each way. Each should then introduce the other to the group by stating a few key facts that they have discovered, including
  - the person's name
  - one thing they are particularly proud of
  - one thing not many people know about him or her
  - one thing he or she hopes to get out of this training.

  By carefully observing reactions, including facial expressions, changes in posture or signs of boredom or interest, you can start to see which individuals may need extra encouragement to participate and which may need careful management to prevent them from dominating the group.
- Share insights with the learners at the beginning. Using the Learning Styles Questionnaire and then discussing the results can provide an interesting and illuminating early exercise for learners if you have the time. It also gives them some language with which to explain their own and other people's behaviour. Belbin's team roles, the Myers-Briggs Type Indicator personality inventory and other analyses of personal style can fulfil a similar function.
- Establish ground rules for behaviour, in small group sessions and plenary discussion. Although best done early, it can be done at any stage, particularly if the group is becoming dysfunctional. Ask the group what rules they want to work by and flipchart their responses. With some coaching to make sure that they cover basic disciplines, interpersonal behaviour and general commitment, they will probably come up with a list that includes things like:

> we will
>> start at 8.30 each morning
>> arrive on time
>> listen to each other
>> give feedback constructively
>> not smoke in the training room
>> switch off mobile phones
>> keep our discussions confidential
>> forget status
>> stick to break times
>> not interrupt each other
>> ration air time so that no one hogs the discussion
>> not go into the office before we start
>> not try to score points off each other.

If any of the listed behaviours start disappearing, you can draw attention to the list and ask every-one to review how they are doing against it. If a behaviour which is not on the list starts to be dis-ruptive – perhaps two people arguing unproductively with the trainer or each other – stop and ask 'What is happening here? Do you want to add anything to your list?'

- Encourage the group to think about the learning process, their own behaviour and what is and is not working for them as a group. Try asking them to comment on the 'how' as well as the 'what' they have arrived at by way of conclusions from group exercises and discussions, and suggest that they note any particularly helpful or unhelpful behaviour.

- Bring issues into the open. If during discussions, practical exercises or other sessions it becomes apparent that someone's behaviour or seniority is getting in the way of his or her own or other peo-ple's learning, you cannot ignore it. Include discussion of such issues as part of the feedback process – see *Giving feedback* below.

The basic principles to follow in managing the dynamics of the group are:

DO:
- Encourage them to take responsibility for how they work together.
- Share insights with the group.
- Have a range of methods to suit different learning styles – to enable each learner to be fully involved.

DON'T:
- Allow preoccupation with learning objectives and tasks to override the need to keep everyone on board in the learning process.
- Be frightened to involve the group in identifying behaviour and its consequences.

GIVING FEEDBACK

Knowledge of results is, as we saw in the first section of this chapter, an important component of learning. Often the feedback from the task itself is sufficient to let the learners know whether they are on the right track. If, for instance, I hit a tennis ball and it lands outside the court, I will know I did something wrong. I will not necessarily know what I did wrong. If, however, my awareness of the connection between my actions and their outcomes has been raised by questions focusing on how it felt when I struck the ball and what I noticed about its flight, I may well be able to adjust the position of my feet, the height of my backswing or whatever else is detracting from my performance. This increase in self-awareness through coaching is a key aspect of effective feedback.

The key steps in the process are:

1 Ask the participants what they saw as their goal(s) in the activity overall and at particular points.
2 Ask them what they did and what they noticed about the effect it had on achievement of their goal(s).
3 Ask them what options they considered to help them achieve their goal(s).
4 Ask them how they decided on a particular option and what criteria they applied.
5 Ask them how the choice of that option has brought them closer to their goal(s).
6 Ask them what, on reflection, if anything, they think they might have done differently, and what effect that might have had on their achievement of the goal(s).

Other forms of feedback can come from external observation – by other learners or from the trainer. To make sure that participants take responsibility for their own learning and to make the feedback a time for reflection rather than for defending past actions, contributions from external sources should not be sought until after the participants have had the chance to review their own performance through the six steps outlined above. When external feedback is sought, the ground rules should be:

DO:
- Make sure that all feedback is clearly related to the objectives of the session and the particular goals the participants were trying to reach.
- Focus on objective observation. 'When you asked the "candidate" whether she planned to have children, she rolled her eyes towards the ceiling' gives an account of observed behaviour more constructively than 'I don't think you should have asked her about having children.'
- Make sure each comment is evidence-based.
- Identify alternative positive behaviours (APBs). 'I wonder what effect it would have had if you had asked him for a specific example when he told you he had lots of experience of project management' suggests what the 'interviewer' might have done more constructively than 'You let him get away with claiming experience of project management.'

DON'T:
- As trainer, be tempted to jump in with your own observations until the group have exhausted theirs. If you do, participants may be tempted to fall back into the habit of seeing you as the main focus, not their own learning.

Sometimes learners will find it helpful to have written feedback or a recording to reflect on later. If the feedback is to be written, it is best done using a structured pro forma to address questions about what did and did not happen and the observed effects. This then provides the learner with a factual account which can be looked at against a checklist of intended behaviour for the task in question.

CASE STUDY

Feedback on perspectives

Following a series of complaints from unsuccessful job applicants, one local authority set up a programme of interview skills training. The trainer was concerned to make sure that interviews were properly planned and structured, that the questions asked were worded appropriately and that the assessment of candidates was soundly-based. She did not want to take responsibility away from the learners, though, and believed the training would have more lasting effects if they were encouraged to develop their own approach rather than being told what to do. She therefore began each phase of the training by asking learners to brainstorm a list of Do's and Don'ts. She recorded all their ideas on a flipchart without comment, and then asked them to think about whose point of view they wanted to look at this from – and why. They agreed that they needed to consider both the interviewer and the interviewee's perspective. They decided to work in smaller groups to identify six of the Do's which they felt were particularly important to help candidates get a realistic view of the job and the organisation, and six which were key to enabling the interviewer to assess the candidate objectively against the specification. When they came back together to compare notes, they quickly agreed their own 'checklist of effective interview behaviour'. The trainer then used role-play with potential 'applicants' to enable the learners to put their ideas into practice.

How do you think they would have structured the feedback afterwards?

SUMMARY: QUICK TIPS

In this chapter we have focused on five different training methods as well as issues to think about before you start (barriers to learning and creating the right climate) and after each phase of activity (giving feedback).

Whichever method(s) you are using,

DO:
■ Identify things that may get in the way – take steps to address them before you start and keep monitoring during the session to take remedial action if needed.
■ Always aim to start where the learners are.
■ Develop a language of learning with the learners. Ideally, this should be based on completion of a Learning Styles Inventory. Engage learners in thinking about the process of learning as well as its content.
■ Recognise your own biases and prejudices.
■ Use coaching, in conjunction with other methods, to raise awareness and foster learner ownership and responsibility.
■ Be clear about the purpose of each method/exercise/phase of training.
■ Build regular feedback opportunities into the process to ensure knowledge of results.

DON'T:
■ Use methods you are not skilled in using.
■ Use methods just for the sake of it.

Assessment

CHAPTER 7

When you have read this chapter you should be able to:

- list at least five different methods of post-course assessment and explain the type of learning objective each might most appropriately be used to test

- explain two benefits for the learner, and two for the employer, of valid post-course assessment.

WHAT IS ASSESSMENT, AND WHY IS IT DONE?

Assessment is the name given to any task or activity designed to test the learner's knowledge, skills, attitudes or competence and allow judgements to be made about the learning that has taken place. Results are normally expressed either as a grade – relating to specific criteria – or as a percentage of possible right answers. A pass mark may be set and learners who fail to achieve it may be required to re-sit or asked to move to other work. The pass mark is best set at a level known to differentiate between those who will perform satisfactorily in the workplace and those who will not – see *Predictive validity* below.

(Assignments are not the same as assessments although similar tasks may be set for each. Assignments are pieces of work undertaken either in groups or individually purely as part of the learning process. Any feedback will be developmental, not judgemental.)

Assessment has three main purposes:

- to provide learners with knowledge of results and feedback while the learning process is in train, to enable them to gauge their progress and identify additional work/effort required

- to enable the trainer to judge whether the pace of training is too fast or too slow, and whether essential prior knowledge and skills are in place

- to make sure that money spent on training has produced the desired results – through systematic evaluation of learning outcomes. We consider evaluation in detail in Chapter 8, but one aspect of it has to do with making sure that learners have learnt what they were intended to learn. This is where assessment comes in.

Assessment which forms part of the learning process is sometimes referred to as *formative*. This is an apt description both in that it helps to move the learner forward, and in that it begins to build a picture of the overall capability of the learner. *Summative* assessment, on the other hand, usually takes place at the end of a programme or phase or module, and brings together an overview of what the learner has achieved. It is this assessment which then informs the evaluation of learning outcomes. Summative assessment may also form the basis of external accreditation and the award of a qualification – see Chapter 3.

If assessment is to be used to gauge progress, it is desirable that it should be carried out both before training takes place (pre-course assessment) and after (post-course assessment). The same test, or a test which is designed to measure the same things, should be used for both.

RELIABILITY AND VALIDITY

Assessment takes many forms, dictated by what is to be assessed. We will consider the assessment of knowledge, skills, attitudes and overall competence in turn. First it is important to make some general points about the design and use of assessment.

To be of any value, assessments must be both reliable and valid.

Reliability

This is the extent to which a test produces consistent results each time it is used. Unless it does, its value is questionable. Reliability is affected not only by the design of the test but also by the conditions under which it is administered. A group of learners sitting a written test paper in a noisy room with lots of distractions are not likely to perform as well as a group who are better able to concentrate – even though in reality both groups may have similar grasp of the knowledge being assessed. It is particularly important that tests reliably measure the performance of all the learners, regardless of race, gender, ethnic origin or disability.

CASE STUDY

Putting it down to experience

At the end of an introduction to machine operations, the trainer asked the learners to write a brief list of Do's and Don'ts when starting up a particular machine. The test backfired when the learner who had shown the most practical ability in starting up the machine failed the test. Because English was not her first language, she struggled to write her response. She could do the task in practice and describe each step to be taken, but she could not write it down.

What should the trainer have done?

Validity

Validity has several facets.

Face validity

This is the extent to which the test 'looks right' to the trainees. If it does not, they will be sceptical about its relevance and its value. It might well be argued that the written test in the above case study would lack face validity to a group of learners who needed only to be able to operate the equipment, not to write about it. If a test lacks face validity, learners may do it half-heartedly or not at all. You can ascertain face validity by asking learners if they can see the relevance of the assessment.

Content validity

It is seldom possible to assess everything the learners should have mastered. The test will inevitably have to provide just a sample of behaviour from which the trainer must base a judgement on the capability of the learners and their readiness to move on to the next phase of learning or out into the workplace. If the sample chosen lacks content validity, it will not be a helpful basis for that judgement.

CASE STUDY

Watching the program

A group of employees had been learning to use tables in Microsoft Word and spreadsheets in Microsoft Excel to enter and manipulate data on their PCs. They were also expected to understand when the use of each was appropriate. When it came to the assessment, they were just asked to input data onto a spreadsheet. Although that was one important element of the training, the trainer could not deduce from their performance of this task whether they also understood when and how to use Word tables and manipulate data. The content sampled was too narrow.

How might the trainer have assessed performance in this case?

Construct validity

This is the extent to which the test measures what it sets out to measure. In the above example, the test should have set out to measure 'constructs' or issues such as the organisation of data. If learners could pass the test simply by entering all their data into the first cell that appeared on the screen, the test would have measured data entry, not data organisation. The wrong construct will have been measured. Likewise with our first example. The construct to be measured is practical, but the assessment was in fact measuring written ability.

Predictive validity

This is the extent to which performance in the test predicts performance in the job. The trainer's role, as we have seen, is not just about enabling learning – it is about ensuring that learning can be transferred back to the workplace. If the results of the test bear no relation to how the learner will operate outside the training room, the training – and the trainer – will quickly become discredited. It is therefore vital to understand the sort of criteria against which performance in the job will be measured. These are the criterion data. They may include speed of operation, customer complaints, error rates or other issues reflected in the standards of performance determined for the job (see Chapter 2). To establish the relationship between performance in the test and performance on the job, either of two alternative approaches can be used:

- *The sealed envelope technique* is where learners undertake the test and their results are kept secret. Once they have been back at work for a while, their assessment results are compared against their performance on the relevant criterion data to see if there is any statistical correlation between the two sets of results.

CASE STUDY

Checkout feedback

In a large retail organisation, learners were taught to use a point-of-sale terminal and were tested in its use before being allowed out onto the shop floor. Those who were fastest and made fewest errors in training were placed in the busiest departments. Unfortunately, the test had not taken into account the pressures of working with a queue of impatient customers and a high proportion of goods with missing bar-codes. A disproportionate number of the 'best' trainees subsequently received poor appraisals from their managers because they were unable to cope with the demands of the job.

Did the test have predictive validity? How could it have been improved?

■ *Concurrent testing* is where a group of current job-holders sit the test. Their results on the test are compared with their on-the-job criterion data to see if the more competent performers do better – ie whether it looks as though the test would have predicted their superior performance.

METHODS OF ASSESSMENT

The methods used for assessment differ depending on what is to be tested.

Assessing knowledge

In *Evaluating Training*, Peter Bramley identifies three levels of knowledge that a learner may require.

Level 1
Facts and basic rules
       Level 2
       Procedures – how things are done and in what sequence
              Level 3
              Analysis – being able to recognise the key features in particular situations and then choose the appropriate procedure from a number of possibilities.

The type of assessment that is appropriate depends on the level of knowledge required. Types include:

■ objective tests
■ open-ended questions
■ assignments and projects.

Objective tests

These may be done orally, using pencil and paper, or on a PC. The learner has to indicate whether a given statement is true or false or whether (a), (b) or (c) is the right answer, by ticking or circling the correct response. Sometimes also described as 'multiple-choice', such tests are relatively quick and easy to mark because a standard grid or score-sheet can be used. They do not require that learners possess any particular level of written ability, although reading skills are needed. They are not as easy to devise as may at first sight appear, because the questions must be worded carefully to avoid giving clues. The usual format consists of a 'stem' statement with four or five responses to choose from. Bramley gives some guidelines for writing this sort of test. These include:

■ Stems should be clear and brief.
■ Stems should not include negatives.
■ Stems should not give clues by using key words which are repeated in the correct answer.
■ Incorrect alternatives (distracters) should be plausible and arranged in a random order so that the correct answer cannot be guessed from its position in the sequence.
■ Questions which require a similar style of response should be grouped together so that the instructions can be simple..

Objective tests are most often used at levels 1 and 2 of the hierarchy of knowledge, although they can be used at level 3. They lend themselves particularly well to online question-and-answer sessions with instant feedback to the learner about whether answers are correct.

For example:

An **anemometer** *measures*

> (a) water pressure
> (b) wind speed
> (c) temperature
> (d) air pressure
> (e) the density of liquids.

Open-ended questions

These are where the learner is asked to list some facts, describe a procedure or analyse alternatives, depending on the level of knowledge to be assessed. Questions should be clear and succinct and guide the learner to the level of detail expected. Examples include:

> *List **three** reasons . . .*
>
> *Briefly describe . . .*
>
> *Explain in not more than **100** words . . .*

Such tests are relatively easy to set but may pose some additional and inappropriate challenges for those whose written skills are not well-developed. They are also harder to mark than objective tests and lend themselves less readily to computer scoring because learners express their answers in different ways. Some software is now available to search for and recognise key words, but otherwise knowledge of the subject is needed to assess whether or not the response is correct. Reliability can be an issue where more than one person is involved in marking.

Assignments and projects

These can be used to assess knowledge at the third, analytical level. Learners can be set a problem or a situation to analyse and asked to produce a report – to include their conclusions about the situation and their recommendations for action. If they are also asked to state any assumptions they are making, this sort of assessment helps to find out whether the learners have grasped the basic principles of the subject and of any associated procedures as well as to test their analytical skills.

Following one management development programme, for example, learners were asked to review the behaviour of their own staff and comment on its implications for the implementation of a planned change programme. Their reports demonstrated the extent to which they had understood what the change programme was to entail, their understanding of employee motivation and behaviour, and their ability to see the implications of one for the other.

Such projects can be tackled either individually or in groups, with the output taking the form of either a written report or an oral presentation. The problems associated with marking open-ended questions are more pronounced with this kind of assessment. The trainer must be very clear what is to be assessed and what constitutes an acceptable response.

Assessing skills

The assessment of practical skills can again take place on several levels:

- basic recognition of steps to be taken – without this, it will be hard for skill to develop at all
- the performance of simple routine procedures, supported by notes or checklists. Simple mechanical tasks – like checking tyre pressures, or things that lend themselves to step-by-step instruction, like using a fire extinguisher – provide examples. In such cases there is a procedure to follow but the level of skill required is fairly rudimentary

- the carrying out of skilled actions that require practice to perfect. These may rely on psychomotor skills, like changing an exhaust, or interpersonal skills, like making a presentation or conducting an interview

- judging whether a piece of skilled work is of an acceptable quality. It is increasingly common for individual employees to have to take responsibility for the quality of their own work. At this highest level of skill, the learners must be able to judge for themselves whether the work done is fit for the purpose.

Because skills at all four levels are about practical activity, the most appropriate form of test is a practical one. Skills can be tested in either of two main ways:

- observation of the process
- review of the outcome.

Observation of the process

This is where the learners are set a task and the trainer watches them perform. An appropriate observation checklist or marking pro forma should be used to note where and when errors are made or the learner deviates from the approved procedure. For customer-service training, for example, the trainer might use a role-play in which one learner is asked to meet and greet a customer, assess the customer's needs, identify a range of product options, handle objections, and close the sale. The marking schedule might look something like the one in Table 22 – although it would be possible to break each of the tasks down into yet finer detail.

Table 22   *Marking schedule for sales tasks*

Task/element	Yes	No	Notes
1 Greets customer politely			
2 Establishes rapport			
3 Asks 'How may I help?'			
4 Establishes what customer wants			
5 Presents relevant products			
6 Explains product features and benefits			
7 Demonstrates product(s)			
8 Encourages customer to handle product(s)			
9 Deals with objections			
10 Closes the sale			
11 Offers appropriate product-care advice			

Review of the outcome

Rather than watch every learner throughout the task, it will often be sufficient just to look at the outcome. Instead of watching all the learners work their way through the creation of a spreadsheet, checking whether each manoeuvre is done by the most efficient method, it may be enough just to time the test and examine the output.

99

This is not a satisfactory approach where the assessment is formative and the trainer needs to give feedback to improve performance because it may not be clear where the learner could have saved time or done things differently. It will, however, save the trainer time and may be useful for an end-of-training summative assessment, provided a set standard for the output has been devised and the trainer knows how to recognise it. To ensure this, trainers themselves must be trained to establish a common standard.

One of the best means of doing this is to ask all the trainers to observe the same live or recorded practical test being carried out by different learners. The trainers can then agree which aspects of what they saw were acceptable and which were not. The results can be captured in a marking schedule like the one shown as Table 22.

Assessing attitudes

These are a lot more difficult to observe than skills. They have to do with feelings, values and beliefs which may only reveal themselves through particular behaviour. Again there are two broad approaches, one designed to assess attitudes across a broad front, the other focusing on the learners' attitudes towards themselves and their belief in their ability to do a particular task to the required standard.

Attitude surveys

If training is being used as part of an organisational change programme, it will be important to test opinions on key aspects of organisational life before and after the training, and possibly during it. Attitude surveys can be constructed using a variety of formats. These are described in detail by Peter Bramley in *Evaluating Training*. The most common styles are illustrated in Figure 4.

Attitudes to self

The perception that one can carry out a particular task successfully is called self-efficacy or self-confidence. Self-efficacy has been shown to be a good predictor of performance. This is probably, according to Bramley, because it is associated with willingness to try something and with persistence in the face of difficulty. It can be measured, before, during and after training, on the basis of self-assessment. The test may be oral, via an interview or focus group conducted by the trainer, or written. Typically, learners are asked to rate, on a scale from one to 10, how confident they are that they can, for example,

- deal with irate customers without losing their temper
- handle an allegation of sexual harassment against one of their team
- interview a prospective customer to assess their wants
- use a particular piece of equipment without assistance
- complete a particular report without errors.

Assessing competence

As we saw in Chapter 2, competence is about more than skills. It is about bringing skills and knowledge to bear to do a task. Assessment of competence is about testing whether or not learners are effective in performing particular tasks. It can best be done via direct observation or the use of assignments and projects.

Following the presentation of the reports in the management development example quoted above, for example, learners were asked to role-play explaining the planned changes to their staff. Their approach was observed by the trainer and fellow-learners using a pre-agreed pro forma describing the required behaviours.

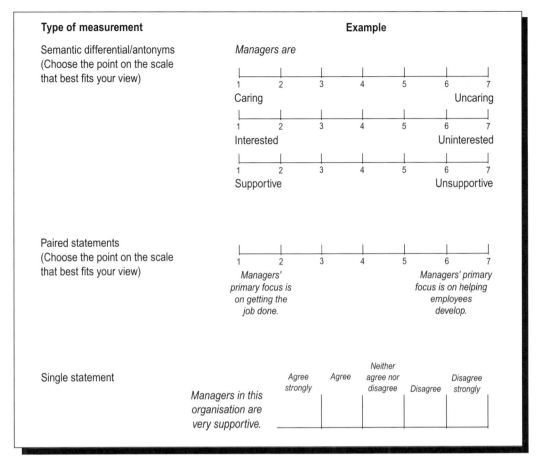

Figure 4   *Approaches to attitude testing*

The behaviours included:

- shows awareness of a range of methods of describing change
- shows understanding of the particular model of change to be used
- empathises with employees and is able to see issues and problems from employees' point of view
- creates compelling vision of the benefits of change
- uses reasoned argument to convince others of the need for change.

Assessment of competence can take place during or at the end of the training or back at the workplace, using the same range of methods as were used in the original identification of needs considered in Chapter 2.

SCHEDULING, MARKING AND RECORDING PROGRESS

Whatever the nature of the objectives the training is designed to serve, and whatever form of assessment has been selected, there are three more aspects of assessment we should consider:

- scheduling of assessment
- marking and feedback
- recording progress.

Scheduling of assessment

We have indicated that assessment, and the insight into learners' progress that it gives, are a valuable part of the learning process. It might even be argued that assessment can be used as a substitute for input. Learners who are constantly attempting structured tests of the sort outlined above are constantly having their awareness raised. More usually, however, assessment and training each play a role. Where this is the case, it is important that learners

- understand the assessment timetable and can cope with it, especially if they need time to prepare for assessment
- feel that they have had an adequate chance to acquire the skills, knowledge or competences to be tested
- have adequate time to carry out the assessment itself.

Depending on the length of the training programme, it is often helpful to schedule an assessment early on. This enables learners to get used to what is expected of them and helps them to feel that they are on the way to achieving the learning objectives and, if applicable, their qualification. If this is not practicable, a formal assignment could be used instead.

Marking and feedback

The importance of a planned and structured approach to marking cannot be over-emphasised. Unless the criteria on which judgements are to be based are clear and explicit, learners will struggle to perform to the required standard. Marking schemes not only save trainer time but also help to ensure consistency of standards. The principles of feedback discussed in Chapter 6 are also important. The trainer's role is to build on the strengths that learners have developed while helping them focus on aspects that need further development. Feedback following formal assessment should

- be clear
- be explicit
- provide suggested alternatives
- where practicable, be written down so that the learner can reflect on it and is in no doubt about what is needed to improve the mark or grade.

Recording progress

If assessment is to count towards an externally accredited programme, all assessments, whether formative or summative, must be carefully tracked. Even where external accreditation has not been sought, the systematic recording of learners' performance in tests may be required to assist in placing trainees in roles which are appropriate to their level of capability or as an input to the evaluation of training – see Chapter 9.

There are many possible formats you can use, and for accredited qualifications a particular one is likely to be prescribed by the Awarding Body. The example in Table 23 provides a basic framework for making sure that you know how each learner is doing at each stage. The weakest stand out at a glance, helping to pinpoint where most attention is needed.

Table 23 *Tracking sheet*

Performance indicator	Name							
	Archie Craven %	Paul Duggan %	Mary Holt %	Jo Roberts %	Rudi Mital %	Sam Patel %	Suzi Gunter %	Jane West %
Word processes letters from hand-drafted text	80	70	65	47	58	75	65	68
Word processes letters from audio dictation	75	70	60	45	55	78	69	70
Imports text into reports	75	75	65	45	60	75	65	72
Imports graphics into reports	80	70	65	40	55	65	70	55

Subject to compliance with the requirements of the Data Protection Act, see Chapter 1, the data can be kept on computer to help build a competence-based profile of each employee.

SUMMARY: QUICK TIPS

DO:
- Make sure you know why you are assessing performance – for the learners' benefit, for your own as trainer, for the organisation, or for all three.
- Tailor the assessment process to the nature of the intended learning – knowledge, skills, attitudes or competences.
- Make sure your assessments are reliable, valid and do not discriminate unfairly.
- Schedule assessments at appropriate points in the programme – starting early but avoiding overloading the learners by doing too many at once.
- Give feedback constructively.
- Keep careful records of progress.

Designing training programmes

TYPES OF TRAINING PROGRAMME

We have not, in previous chapters, tried to distinguish between one-off learning events to meet specific objectives and training programmes. In this chapter we focus on the latter.

A training programme is a series of linked events designed, when completed, to equip people with the range of competencies needed to do a whole job.

Training programmes may be mounted using exclusively on-the-job or exclusively off-the-job learning, or a combination of both. They may also involve internal or external providers, or both. Some are relatively short in duration. It may take an induction programme lasting only a few days to introduce an already competent recruit into a relatively small organisation. Others may last several years. Some senior management development programmes incorporating study for an MBA, internal and external secondments and projects and specific career moves would fall into the second category.

In this chapter we consider a few of the most common. You may encounter others – but the trainer's role is likely to remain broadly similar. Specifically we will look at:

- common features
- induction programmes
- technical and professional training programmes and Modern Apprenticeships
- management and supervisory schemes
- individual programmes.

COMMON FEATURES

Most types of programme have the following in common:

- *multiple linked objectives*, often but not always relating to a group rather than one person. 'What are the competencies needed to become an effective branch manager?' is a more likely starting point than 'How can we help branch managers to utilise all the functions of the new point-of-sale equipment?'

- *a combination of learning methods* – and perhaps providers. In some instances the programme will be largely on-the-job with courses or other off-the-job events relatively few and far between. In others, in particular those linked to qualifications, the off-the-job elements may effectively determine the work to be done between courses

- some form of *programme management* to ensure that each element is planned at an appropriate point in the learning sequence and takes place as scheduled

- *regular reviews of progress* to ensure that each element, and the programme as a whole, is delivering the required learning, and to ensure that each trainee is progressing as expected. Learners who fall behind or fail to make the grade may be removed from the programme

- (generally) an expectation that *the programme will be undertaken by more than one learner*, either simultaneously or over time. There are exceptions – where an induction programme is specifically tailored to the needs of one person, or where a particular individual is being groomed for a specific role. We consider these shortly.

The main steps involved are outlined in Figure 5 and explained in more detail below.

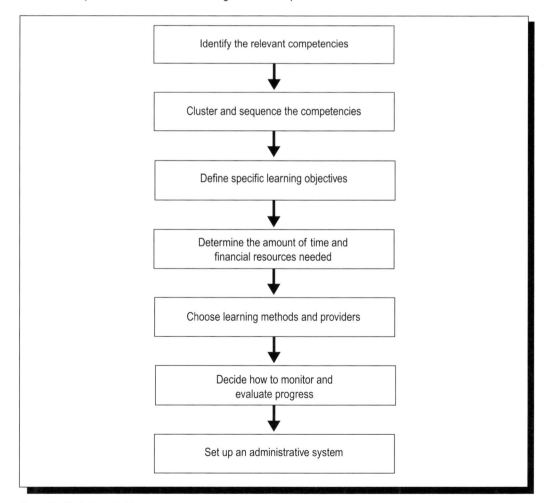

Figure 5   *Designing a training programme*

Identify the relevant competencies

In Chapter 2 we reviewed some ways of identifying competencies needed in particular roles. This must be the starting point for any programme intended to prepare people for those roles. Whether the goal is to produce a 'cadre' of supervisors, technical experts or general managers, the programme cannot take shape until the designer has a clear and hopefully accurate picture of what these roles involve and what it takes to perform effectively in them.

Cluster and sequence the competencies

The competencies must be clustered and sequenced in order to identify the possible shape of the overall programme. Trainees will not be able to master everything at once. Some aspects may be linked by common concepts or skills. Mastery of some may depend on having first mastered others. Programmes which have been run in the same form for many years may need review to make sure these internal relationships are still valid.

Define specific learning objectives

Specific learning objectives should be set for each aspect, to define the standard of performance required – see Chapter 2.

Determine the amount of time and financial resources needed

Time and resources may have to be 'negotiated' to produce an appropriate cost-benefit payback. Some managers are wary of long and elaborate programmes which appear to cost a lot and provide little return beyond an impressive CV for participants. Others take a more philosophical view.

Choose learning methods and providers

Choose learning methods and providers – see Chapters 3 and 6 – with the twin aims of providing an effective means of achieving each objective and providing an appropriate mix of approaches.

Decide how to monitor and evaluate progress

Decide how to monitor and evaluate progress – for individuals, each cohort of learners, and the programme overall. In some cases the formality of examinations may be appropriate, during or at the end of the programme. In others, some form of self-review, maybe with a learning log or diary in which trainees note key learning outcomes – see Chapter 11 – may be better.

INDUCTION PROGRAMMES

Whenever a new recruit joins, there are likely to be new things to learn. Some of these may be common to all:

- the organisation's vision and values
- the organisation's objectives
- who's who in the organisation
- what to do in the event of fire or an accident
- holiday and sickness arrangements
- organisational rules of conduct
- standard procedures – payment of salaries, expense claims, etc.

Others will be specific to particular departments:

- the location of fire exits
- the names of first aiders
- departmental objectives
- who's who in the department
- specific hours of work, meal breaks and rules of conduct.

Yet others will be unique to the job. The size of this last category will depend on how the skills and knowledge required differ from those the recruit already has. Even if the gap is narrow, the working processes are unlikely to be identical, and the people and locations involved are certainly different. The size of the difference determines the amount of training that will be needed.

In some cases the trainer may have been involved in recruitment. This is particularly likely where there are specific training schemes – for management, technical or other trainees (see below). In that case the induction programme is often common to all those entering the scheme. For other recruits, the trainer is more likely to work with the personnel department, if there is one, and the recruiting manager to tailor a general programme to individual needs. Developing an induction programme involves the tasks listed in Table 24.

Table 24 *Induction tasks*

Task	Process
Researching the needs of people new to the company	May involve interviewing recent recruits to find out how relevant and useful they found their own induction and how they feel about the timing, pace and methods used
Reviewing the effectiveness of existing induction	May involve talking to line managers, interviewing leavers, or analysing the employee turnover and performance of those who have recently joined
Examining other organisations' induction programmes	Making a comparison with your own company's scheme – perhaps through a formal benchmarking process
Undertaking a detailed job analysis – see Chapter 2	Identifying the component tasks of particular jobs, the competencies required, and hence the key elements to be addressed during initial training

In constructing the programme itself it is important to get the right mix of on- and off-the-job learning. Too much of the latter and the new recruit many feel frustrated that he or she has not 'got started on a proper job'.

It is also important to involve the right people – preferably those the new recruits needs to know – like the MD or the general manager or their own boss – and to use the right mix of methods. Particularly where recruits will go through a standard programme one or two at a time it is tempting to manage some of the delivery through videos/DVD or other remote media. Although this has its place, it may not be what the newcomer will most value. In the first few disorienting weeks of a new job, personal contact and the knowledge that 'someone cares' may provide a firmer foundation for the employment relationship than a few hi-tech messages from senior managers. A buddy system by which experienced employees partner the new recruits, shows them around, introduces them to others and answers their questions, can be useful here.

The trainer's role in operating the induction programme could range from planning and co-ordinating it to actually delivering it. In some organisations, the apparently routine nature of induction means that even those relatively inexperienced in training may be asked to manage the programme or conduct elements of it. Others recognise the vital importance of first impressions and involve only their most experienced trainers. It is pointless to spend hundreds – even thousands – of pounds on recruitment only to turn people off through inept induction.

TECHNICAL AND PROFESSIONAL TRAINING PROGRAMMES AND MODERN APPRENTICESHIPS

Some organisations offer a limited number of training places each year to help ensure that there will always be enough people coming through the business competent in core activities. Engineering firms, for example, may offer technical traineeships and firms of accountants or lawyers offer professional traineeships.

Table 25   *Possible trainer involvement in technical and professional programmes*

Trainer activity	Explanation
Design	Working with specialists inside and outside the organisation to design a programme with the right mix of current practice, future developments and leading-edge thinking
Investigating funding	Determining what funding/financial support might be available for all or part of the programme, especially if it is geared to attaining an NVQ. The local Learning and Skills Council (LSC) is the first port of call
Negotiating funding	Discussion with external providers and funding bodies such as the LSC
Administration	Seeing to funding or attendance arrangements
Recruitment	Assisting either in an administrative capacity – placing advertisements, organising interviews and assessment days and the associated correspondence with candidates – or as a selector yourself
Monitoring	Scrutinising the programme, including trainee attendance and standards achieved
Acting as counsellor to the trainees	Being someone they can turn to for advice if they are finding things difficult or whose help they can seek in, for example, getting more support from their line manager in the on-the-job elements
Acting as 'placement officer'	Finding suitable projects or secondments for trainees. These may be internal or external and will involve making sure that both sides understand the terms of reference and each other's expectations. You may also fulfil a similar role at the end of the programme if it is necessary to act as 'broker' for first appointments with line managers who may not know any of the trainees well
Evaluating the programme	Assessment in the medium and long term. This could mean undertaking detailed analytical work tracking the career and salary progression of former trainees to identify retention and promotion rates, and seeing whether the programme overall is achieving its goals

Sometimes entry to such schemes is drawn directly from schools, colleges or universities. Sometimes it is open to more experienced candidates from inside or outside the business. Sometimes schemes are designed and operated on the basis of the requirements of a single company. Sometimes consortia will join together and involve colleges, universities or other external providers in delivery. Occasionally, sandwich courses at university form an integral part of the programme. Sometimes programmes lead to an externally-recognised qualification. Sometimes a company certificate or diploma is awarded. Sometimes 'graduation' to a particular role or level in the organisation marks the end of the programme.

Unless you are a technical expert in your own right, you are not likely to be directly involved in conducting such programmes. But you are likely to have a role in their management or administration. Modern Apprenticeships, which were discussed in Chapter 1, require a considerable amount of administrative support. Especially where LSC funding is involved, careful records of plans, payments, progress and achievement must be kept. The progress of individual trainees must be carefully monitored and close contact maintained with all the other parties. You may be involved in any or all of the ways outlined in Table 25 above, and will be subject to inspection every four years by the Adult Learning Inspectorate.

MANAGEMENT AND SUPERVISORY TRAINING SCHEMES

These, like technical and professional schemes can be run wholly internally or partly externally. They may or may not entail work towards formal qualifications. Some organisations have several such schemes, ranging from a senior-manager- or even director-level development programme down to direct entry schemes for those with level 3 qualifications – see Chapter 1 – or degrees. We will focus on the more junior end of this spectrum.

The length and content of such programmes varies, as do the expectations of the participants regarding their medium- and long-term career destinations. In many organisations, graduate schemes in particular have had a somewhat chequered history.

- When times are hard, recruitment may be cut back or even stopped altogether.

- Those who joined the organisation to do a job rather than to get on a 'fast-track' scheme sometimes resent their high-profile colleagues – leading some employers to offer access to existing employees as well as those fresh from the education system.

- The difficulty of predicting potential in candidates in their late teens and early twenties has meant that some schemes have a high dropout rate. Sometimes this is because trainees decide they have made the wrong career choice. Sometimes it is because the employers decide they have selected someone who will not make the grade.

- The nature of management and supervisory roles is changing rapidly in some organisations. Some of those who have come through the scheme may not, after all, be competent to fill key roles in the business tomorrow. This may throw into question the design and content of the whole programme.

As a trainer concerned to ensure the future as well as the present skill base of your organisation, you will need constantly to question the objectives of such schemes and their link with other programmes of employee development. With your line management colleagues, and possibly external help, you should check periodically to make sure that the competencies the programme was designed to develop are still relevant to the emerging needs of the organisation. This may impact on

- recruitment to the scheme. Are some degree disciplines more relevant than others? Do some educational establishments produce candidates better suited to your needs? Perhaps someone ought to do some detailed analysis of past intakes to find out

- the expectations you seek to create. Are all your communications with potential recruits realistic and consistent – from the first advertisement in a careers directory or website, through any leaflets or brochures you lodge with careers offices, to the language used by everyone they meet at interview and during other phases of selection – right through the induction process?

- the design of the programme. Are the specific learning objectives of each element clear, explicit and relevant? Is it clear how achievement will be measured at each stage? Are the links between on- and off-the-job components clear and understood by those concerned with each? Research to identify any mismatches could be part of your role. So too could be study of participant reactions to particular parts of the programme

- learning methods. Are these in line with participant expectations? For those who have been used to 24-hour access to PCs for private study using e-learning, a return to a tutor-centred 'chalk and talk' approach could seem quaint or patronising. If it is not what they expected at the start of a high-flying career, they may start looking for a more progressive employer. Even if trainees appear happy to settle back and be 'spoon-fed', you will need to find ways of increasing their self-reliance and responsibility for their own learning. Coaching can be a key element of this

- tutors' styles and approaches. Are you using your brightest and best people to provide role models and inspire commitment? Or are you fielding the second, or even the third, eleven – people who have failed in line management roles or have time on their hands for other reasons – such as impending retirement. Are they providing enough intellectual stimulation – or merely an entertaining diversion?

As well as demanding high standards of design and delivery, management and supervisory trainees are likely to need just the same level of emotional and administrative support as technical trainees. This may extend to help in finding accommodation if they are new to the area. The administration of relocation arrangements could therefore be part of your brief.

As with technical trainees, relationships will have to be established with local providers to arrange day or block release for qualification courses such as the Diploma in Management Studies (DMS) or National Examining Board for Supervision and Management (NEBS Management). If the programme is large enough, a special variant may be tailored for your organisation. This will allow potentially greater flexibility of pace and content. It will, however, deprive your trainees of the chance to mix with those from other organisations – which can be particularly beneficial at this stage in their careers.

INDIVIDUAL PROGRAMMES

These take two main forms:

- tailored versions of general programmes
- unique programmes.

Tailored versions of general programmes

Some organisations modify their technical, professional, management or supervisory training programmes to suit the needs of particular individuals. In such a way a graduate with a business studies degree might skip those parts of the management training programme which would duplicate learning already acquired. In that case, it will be necessary to check the detailed syllabus content and performance criteria to make sure that the trainee will not miss out. It will also be important to weigh up whether it is better for the whole group to follow the training programme together or allow an element of pick-and-mix.

Unique programmes

If your organisation recruits a new chief executive with no experience of your particular industry, neither your planned open training events nor your management or technical training scheme may quite fit the bill to bring him or her up to speed. The depth and breadth of knowledge required, and the speed with which learning will have to take place are likely to be rather different from those of your average trainee. That is not to say that modules from existing training cannot be included or adapted if they fit his or her needs. What it does mean is that the essential elements of what the business is about and how it works at present must be conveyed quickly and effectively. This may require a programme of visits, one-to-one meetings and access to financial reports and business planning documents – rather than any sort of 'course'.

The need for this sort of programme does not arise very often. Much more common is the situation in which an individual is identified as having some, but not all, of the competencies needed for a particular role and wishes to develop the rest. Development centres, which we discussed in Chapter 2, are designed to highlight such instances.

Because each person's profile of competencies is different, each will need an individually tailored programme. This may comprise new on-the-job experiences, perhaps via internal secondment, or coaching to gain more from the existing job. It may also include attendance at specific external programmes – at a national or international business school, perhaps. One or more of the open events in the company training calendar may also be appropriate – or a special course for those with a shared need could be devised.

Whatever the content of the programme, the process for developing it will generally follow the pattern outlined at the beginning of this chapter. In particular, clarity of objectives and of initial expectations is crucial. If the individual believes that success in the training programme will lead to promotion whereas the company believes it may stave off dismissal, there could be problems ahead.

The individual nature of these programmes can pose particular challenges for the trainer – especially when it comes to planning, timetabling and evaluating. It is generally much easier to keep track of 20 people doing 10 things together than of 10 people doing 20 things separately. As so often in training, the efficiency of the administration process could count for as much as the effectiveness of specific learning events.

SUMMARY

- A training programme comprises a series of linked events designed to equip people with the range of competencies needed to do a whole job.
- They may be exclusively on-the-job, exclusively off-the-job, or a mixture, and may include a range of different learning methods.
- Programmes require management and regular review .
- Most will be undertaken by more than one learner, either simultaneously or over time. Individually tailored programmes arising from development centres are one exception to this.
- Designing a programme involves identifying relevant competencies, clustering and sequencing them, defining specific learning objectives, determining resources, choosing learning methods and providers, deciding how to monitor and evaluate, and setting up an administrative system.
- The most common types of programme are:
  - induction
  - technical and professional training schemes and Modern Apprenticeships
  - management and supervisory training schemes

■ Developing an induction programme may entail researching needs, reviewing effectiveness, bench-marking with other companies or undertaking detailed job analysis.

■ The trainer's involvement with technical, professional, management and supervisory programmes may include:
- design
- investigating funding
- negotiating funding
- administration
- recruitment
- monitoring
- acting as counsellor to the trainees
- acting as 'placement officer'
- evaluating the programme.

Review and evaluation

CHAPTER OBJECTIVES

When you have read this chapter you should be able to:

- define what is meant by 'review and evaluation' and describe four different levels at which evaluation can take place

- cite two benefits for the learner, and two for the employer, of effective evaluation

- list at least four different methods of evaluation and describe the circumstances in which each might most appropriately be used.

WHAT IS REVIEW AND EVALUATION, AND WHY IS IT DONE?

Evaluation is the process of establishing the worth of the training that has been carried out. In *Evaluating Training*, Peter Bramley identifies three main purposes:

- *feedback*: to help trainers understand the extent to which objectives are being met and the effectiveness of particular learning activities – as an aid to continuous improvement – see below

- *control*: to make sure that training policy and practice are in tune with organisational goals and delivering cost-effective solutions to organisational issues

- *intervention*: to involve managers and supervisors more actively in the total learning process by engaging them both before and after training has taken place.

It enables three key questions to be answered:

- Did the training achieve its objectives?
- Did it make a difference to the organisation?
- Was it worth the money that was spent on it?

The answers to these questions are important because:

- Ineffective training is not only a waste of time and money, it can also damage the self-esteem of the learners. They may feel it is somehow their fault that they have not been able to master the content of the training. Even if that does not happen, their motivation to undergo future training may be weakened. Training that is ineffective must be re-thought and re-designed if it is to be repeated.

- Training that does not benefit the organisation is a luxury very few managements can afford to tolerate. The benefit need not necessarily be immediate or direct. Sometimes, as we saw in Chapter 1, it will provide one of the building blocks for future capability. But if the link between training and some measure of organisational performance cannot be made, and measured, the training team could well find themselves without much of a future.

- Training that was not worth the money which was spent on it may have produced some results, for either the individual or the organisation as a whole, but not enough to justify the cost. More cost-effective alternatives – in the form of a less expensive or re-designed training programme or changes to recruitment strategy to employ people who already have the required skills – may have to be sought.

Evaluation relies on a systematic review of the process of training as well as assessment of the outcomes it has achieved. For the trainer it is itself a learning process. Training that has been planned and delivered is reflected on. Views of how to do it better are formulated and tested – and built in next time around. The outcome may be to

- abandon the training
- re-design the training – new sequence, new methods, new content, new trainer
- re-design the preparation/pre-work – new briefing material, new pre-course work
- re-think the timing of the training – earlier or later in people's careers, earlier or later in the training programme, earlier or later in the company calendar
- leave well alone.

LEVELS OF EVALUATION

Evaluation can take place at any or all of four different levels.

- the reactions of trainees – ie what they thought of the training
- the learning that has taken place as a result of the training – ie the immediate outcome
- changes in behaviour in the job which follow– ie the intermediate outcome
- the impact on results for the organisation– ie the ultimate outcome.

Reactions level

Evaluation at this level typically takes the form of some sort of 'happy sheet'. This is a somewhat derisory reference to the fact that post-course questionnaires used to gauge reactions tend to paint a rosy picture of the event – often coloured by the quality of the food or the sociability of the delegates.

The format ranges from the relatively simple – 'highlight the best and worst aspects' – to a detailed, session-by-session review and rating of tutor preparation, presentation, content, opportunities for participation and feedback, and so on. Review sheets may be designed specifically for each course or follow a general format. Computer software is now available to generate them automatically on the basis of pre-specified objectives.

Unless learners have a particular reason to return their response sheets or can see any benefit in it for themselves, it is likely that the return rate will be low. As an alternative, and to encourage learners to think objectively about the learning process, a group debriefing at the end of each session or day can serve a similar purpose. This too will benefit from some structure – even if it is only asking learners to list the positives about the experience as well as the negatives, and capturing them on a flipchart as a prelude to probing the views which appear to be the most widely held. Unless handled carefully, though, such sessions may either remain at a very superficial level as learners prepare to quit the training venue, or, if the training has not gone well, degenerate into an unproductive 'bitch and gripe' session.

The benefit of evaluation at this level is that the experience of training is still fresh in learners' minds. Although this may make it harder for them to take an overview or judge how the training may alter their behaviour in the longer term, it does mean that they can help the trainer review which parts of the process felt right and which did not.

Immediate outcome/learning level

We discussed the assessment of learning in Chapter 7. The emphasis there was on assessment as a means of judging how the learners are progressing and what they have achieved. The same information can be used to give an insight into how effective the training has been. If all the learners do well on all the assessments, that would indicate either

■ that the training was effective

or

■ that their training needs were not accurately assessed initially and they already possessed the skills and knowledge which the training was intended to develop.

The use of the sort of pre- and post-course assessment we discussed will help to determine which it is. For only some of the trainees to do well on the assessments could mean that some individuals' needs or their individual learning styles were not accurately assessed. If none of them does well, that could mean

■ the training was ineffective or inappropriate

■ the assessment has not accurately measured the learning that has taken place.

Further research, probably involving the learners themselves, will be needed to find out which it is.

Once you are satisfied that the assessment is a fair reflection of the outcome of training, a review of the process of training can follow. Assuming that there is a clear link between the assessment and the learning objectives, the review of the content and methods used to achieve each objective can focus on any that do not seem to have been met.

Job behaviour/intermediate outcome level

The application and transfer of learning cannot be measured through a post-course test. If training has been carried out in response to a clearly identified need, arising out of the way in which the employee was doing the job before the training, it should be possible to evaluate the training by seeing whether job performance has changed for the better. The range of techniques that helped identify training needs in the first place can be brought into play.

So if the learner is observed at work after the training as well as before, a comparison can be obtained. Test situations can be created at work – before and after training – to see how the learner performs. 'Mystery shoppers' or similar situations can be set up. Routine measures of performance can be analysed to see if there has been any change. Performance appraisal (see Chapter 2) provides an opportunity to take a longer-term view of the part that training has played in bringing about improvements in performance.

Evaluation at this level inevitably tends to focus on the effects of the training as a whole. The review of training content and methods should, in most cases, follow. Once you know which of the learning objectives have been achieved and which have not, you can review the training design in the light of this.

CASE STUDY

Gone off pop

A customer service organisation put all its call centre operators through a programme intended to reduce the number of customer complaints about slow response times. Both actual response times and numbers of complaints were monitored before and after the training programme. On their return from training, operator response times had improved by 10 per cent, but one month later the number of customer complaints had increased by 15 per cent. On further investigation it became apparent that the style of taped music playing while customers were on 'hold' had been changed from classical to 'pop' while the training programme was under way. This irritated some customers and made them feel as though they had been holding on longer.

What conclusions can be drawn about the effectiveness of the training at job performance level?

Although objective measurement against clear performance criteria is important, care must always be taken to ensure that the effects of training can be isolated. A host of other factors, from changes in the product range or delivery arrangements to the weather or England's performance on the cricket pitch could have an impact on customers' propensity to complain.

One way of countering this is to undertake a special review of the learners' confidence and competence at work after an appropriate interval. We saw in Chapter 7 that self-efficacy is an important predictor of performance. If the learner and his or her boss both believe that the training has increased confidence or competence or both, that is a positive outcome. A follow-up questionnaire, issued to learners and their managers with a view to a joint discussion and conclusion, can

- serve as a reminder about the objectives of the training
- rekindle awareness by re-focusing on performance
- help identify any further needs which have not yet been met
- enable the impact perceived by learners and their managers to be evaluated in their own terms
- provide an opportunity for detailed investigation of the parts of the training and the particular methods used which are perceived to have had most and least impact, thereby assisting the review process.

Peter Bramley refers to this as responsive evaluation, when stakeholder views are used to construct a rounded view of the impact of the training. It can also be used, with senior management, at the final level of evaluation.

Results/ultimate outcome level

Assessing the impact of training on the effectiveness with which the organisation as a whole reaches its objectives is among the hardest, but most important, aspects of evaluation. Unless there has been one specific, organisation-wide programme, evaluation at this level will not throw much light on the training process. Instead, it will provide an insight into whether the investment that the organisation makes in training appears to be worthwhile. The precise methods used will depend on the nature of the organisation's main goals and the factors it has identified as critical to its successful performance.

One approach is to assess whether there is any statistical correlation between, for instance, employee hours devoted to training and profit, sales turnover, return on capital or other more immediate indicators of business performance, such as the number of customer complaints, number of rejects, level of employee turnover, and so forth.

Evaluation at this level could also entail collating the costs of training (see Chapter 10) and attempting to set these against the value of specific business improvements. In some cases this may be relatively straightforward. Suppose that in order to pitch for a new contract worth £x over one year, six new people were recruited and then trained – at a cost of £y over one year. If x is greater than y, the training was probably worthwhile – depending on the other costs of servicing the contract.

Unfortunately, in most organisations things are less clear-cut. Attributing a specific sales or profit gain solely to training can be very dubious. So many other internal factors – changes of systems, procedures, personnel, and so on – and external factors – the economic climate, competitor activity, market trends, etc – also have a bearing.

That is why some of the other indicators mentioned above can be more useful. The problem then is to work out how much a 5 per cent reduction in customer complaints is actually worth, in the short and medium term. Although methods exist to do this, they usually have to be based on rather a lot of assumptions about customers' life-time buying habits and the impact of complaints on their own and their acquaintances' buying behaviour.

EVALUATION TOOLS

As with the assessment methods considered in Chapter 7, at whatever level the evaluation is carried out, the tools used to do it must be both reliable – producing consistent results – and valid – measuring accurately whether or not objectives have been achieved. Getting good reactions-level evaluations from a group who have just been told they are to receive a bonus or a pay rise is likely to be easier than getting them from learners facing the threat of redundancy.

Some of the tools that can be used at each level of evaluation are shown in Table 26.

Rather than waiting until the training is almost over before you start thinking about evaluation, consider it as an integral part of the training design. As we saw in Chapter 7, it makes sense to do this for assessment – which will inform the immediate learning level evaluation. It also makes sense at the job behaviour level. If you know what changes in behaviour you are seeking to foster, you will be able to articulate the learning objectives more clearly. When determining which method to use,

- Select one appropriate to the level of evaluation you want to conduct.
- Consider whether the necessary resources are available to use a particular method. Issues to consider include:
  - Does anyone have the necessary time, knowledge, skills, for example, to design a questionnaire – or does one come with any training package you are using?
  - Has enough time been allowed at the end of the training for learners to provide reactions-level feedback?
  - Have you considered and agreed how, when, from whom and in what form information to evaluate at job performance and organisation levels will be available?
  - Are the resources available for analysis of the data collected for evaluation?

Table 26 *Tools for evaluation*

Tools	Level			
	Reactions	Learning	Behaviour	Results
Delegate questionnaires or reports	✓	✓	✓	✓
Manager questionnaires or reports	✓	✓	✓	✓
Written test or examination		✓		
Practical test or demonstration		✓	✓	
Customer survey – postal/online – focus groups			✓	✓
Employee survey – postal/online – focus groups			✓	✓
Interviews	✓	✓	✓	✓
Performance appraisal (360-degree appraisal)		✓	✓	
Observation		✓	✓	
Company financial results				✓
Company results on other relevant performance indicators				✓
Results on team/departmental performance indicators				✓
Results on personal performance indicators			✓	✓
Top management opinion	✓	✓	✓	✓
Recognition as an Investor in People				✓

- Decide whether the costs of the proposed evaluation arrangements are proportionate to the costs and scale of the training itself. A half-day customer care session for six new recruits out of a staff of 100 will hardly warrant setting up a dedicated website on which all customers are asked for feedback about the standard of customer care received. If on the other hand the website already exists and all six of the staff are involved with a particular product or geographical area, it would probably be relatively easy to channel the relevant customers to provide feedback

- Be clear how the results of evaluation should be interpreted. How high should standards be set? Should the trainer who receives 100-per-cent positive feedback from 50 per cent of the delegates and 100-per-cent negative feedback from the other half, draw the same conclusions as the one who gets 50 per cent negative and 50 per cent positive from everyone? The answer is probably not. But without knowing a lot more about the characteristics of the trainers and the nature of the feedback, it would be hard to decide which should carry more weight.

■ Make sure you know what you will do with the results of the evaluation. Who will be interested in the outcome of the evaluation – just the learners and the trainer, or their managers and senior management? Will you be able to handle the negatives as well as the positives? For the manager who oversees the evaluation of training, this may, for example, mean taking action if a particular trainer receives consistently negative reactions-level evaluations.

SUMMARY: QUICK TIPS

In this chapter we defined evaluation as a process for assessing the worth of training – based on a systematic review of the training itself and the outcomes it has achieved. We considered it at four levels, from the short-term reactions of the learners to the long-term impact on the organisation. For the trainer, we have identified a number of issues to consider, including:

DO:
■ Think of evaluation as more than just a 'happy sheet'. All four levels are important and major programmes should be evaluated at least to job behaviour level to see what impact they have had.
■ Build the evaluation process into the training design rather than tacking it on as an afterthought.
■ Choose a method which suits the level of evaluation you want, and make sure that you have the resources to design the process, to collect the data, to analyse it and then to review the implications for training content and methods.
■ Make sure that there is a commitment to act on the results of evaluation. Unless the findings will be used to improve the quality of training, make it more cost-effective or identify the need for alternative approaches, the cost of the process will outweigh its benefits.

DON'T:
■ Try to do it all yourself. Comprehensive evaluation should involve learners, their managers and colleagues, senior management and sometimes customers, suppliers and external training providers as well.

Management and administration

CHAPTER OBJECTIVES

When you have read this chapter you should be able to:

- identify the factors that influence the resources required by the training function in your organisation

- explain how, and from where, organisations can obtain help with the costs of training

- list four types of question the training department may be asked, and where the answers to each should be found

- list three advantages of computerised training information.

SETTING UP A TRAINING DEPARTMENT

Most of this text so far applies whether or not your organisation has an in-house training department. In this chapter our focus shifts to assume that you have, or that you want to set up, a specialist department.

If you are involved in setting up or formalising the training function, it is important to be clear, from the outset,

- exactly what is expected of you
- what resources you have.

If you are working on the assumption that you have a policy-making, internal consultant's role (see Chapter 1) while everyone else thinks you are there as a service to provide administrative support, you will be doomed to frustration. If, on the other hand, you see your role as purely administrative when senior managers are looking for proactive input to the development of training policy, your career prospects could be bleak.

Much may depend on the reasons for establishing the function in the first place. The organisation may always have invested in training its people – but in an *ad hoc* uncoordinated manner without a clear link to the corporate plan or a coherent strategy for delivering it. In that case, creating an effective, non-bureaucratic framework for existing activity may be all that is needed.

If, on the other hand, learning has previously been through unstructured trial and error on the job, establishing the training function could demand a fundamental change of culture for everyone. Try to get a feel for the size of the task you are being asked to undertake. Establish such basic facts as:

- How many employees are involved?
- What categories of employee are involved?
- What has been the approach to training for each category?

- What has prompted the chief executive or other decision-makers to establish the function now? Is it in response to:
  - a specific one-off failure/mistake?
  - the continuing trend in corporate results?
  - 'flavour of the month' in the media?
  - customers' requesting it as part of an approach to Total Quality Management?
  - a general drive for quality, perhaps in pursuit of industrial quality standards like BS5750 or ISO9002?
  - a desire for recognition as an Investor in People (see Chapter 1)?

- How deeply held and widely shared is the belief in training? (Where the whole management team is eager for change, your task will be different from [and easier than] where doubt and backsliding is the order of the day.)

The answers to questions like these will help to shape your role. The role which you agree initially will not necessarily be permanent. An early emphasis on administration may change to something more proactive as your contribution is established and as the organisation and you develop. Conversely, the trainer who has internal consultancy status to begin with may find the role diminishing over time. This could be because managers are dissatisfied by the quality of your input – or because other functions have begun to seize the initiative.

Your role, and the range and level of activities in which you are expected to become involved, will determine the resources you will need. If you can, negotiate some time to assess exactly what you will require and a chance to review this after, say, six months.

Try to strike a balance when negotiating resources. You will not gain credibility by empire-building. But if you stretch yourself and your people too tightly, something will snap. It is impossible to set down targets for the ratio of trainers to learners. So much depends on the nature of the role, your starting point and the stability of the environment in which you are working. In industries with high employee turnover or particularly complex or dangerous work processes, relatively more resources will be needed per employee.

Start by listing all the activities in which you expect to be involved. Break each down into its component parts and work out roughly

- how long each part takes
- how often it will be repeated.

If, for example, you will be involved in providing induction training for new employees, you could work out how often there are new recruits and hence the number of courses that are likely to be needed. (There may, of course, be a trade-off between the need to induct everyone in all aspects from Day 1 and the possibility of working with larger groups at longer intervals.) You can then calculate

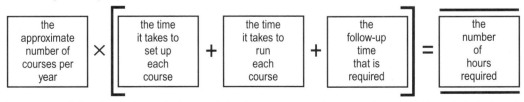

If you can, distinguish between tasks which involve policy, planning, operational activity and clerical work (see Chapter 1). If you repeat this process for each of your areas of involvement, you will begin to get a broad picture of the time – and thus the number of employee hours – you will need.

Some areas of activity are much simpler to assess in these terms than others – hence the advice to negotiate a review period. Once the function is up and running, it is a lot easier to monitor how much time is being spent on particular activities and to modify your estimates accordingly.

Individual task

1   Make a list of all the people available to help you in your training role. Enter their names in the appropriate column of the matrix below.

2   Complete the matrix to indicate the type of contribution they can make.

Name	Contribution				
	Identifying needs	Designing	Delivering	Recording	Evaluating

You will find more discussion of the 'politics' of who to involve in Alison Hardingham's *Designing Training*.

Remember, too, that resources can comprise equipment as well as people. The more you can automate, the fewer people you will need. As we saw in Chapter 4, technology-based learning can have an important contribution to make to the delivery of training and save expensive time at an operational level. Simply by automating the production of the invitations, joining instructions and follow-up documentation, you can save on clerical time. Compare the cost of appropriate software against the salary and employment costs of additional clerical help before you decide.

Only if you get the right balance between people and equipment will you be able to provide an efficient and effective service. Providing an *efficient* service will usually mean being able to provide management and learners with information and well-founded advice, often at short notice. The rest of this chapter is devoted to this. Providing an *effective* service is what the rest of the book has been about.

BUDGETING FOR TRAINING

The costs of external training are relatively easy to calculate. The fees actually charged by the external provider will be readily identifiable. The costs of the learners' time and their travelling and out-of-pocket expenses will have to be added, and there may be additional venue costs. To calculate the full cost even of external training, the costs of management time spent meeting the provider(s), and of identifying needs, and review and evaluation after the event, ought to be added.

Calculating the full cost of in-house training is a more complex task. The simplest way of working out the cost of an individual activity is to take the items listed in Table 27 add them up. The total will be for the particular training course or event, and can be divided by the number of learners participating to give a cost per head – sometimes called a *per capita* cost – or by the number of hours the training lasts to give a cost per training hour.

The most complicated part of the calculation will be working out what we have called the 'trainer charge-out rate'. It would be much simpler just to take the trainer's annual salary and on-costs (National Insurance,

Table 27   *In-house training costs*

Item	Method of calculation	£
Trainer time	Trainer's hourly charge-out rate *x* number of hours devoted to design, delivery and evaluation of event	
Venue	Invoiced amount (if external venue); if internal, proportion of annual rent, rates and utilities bills (based on number of square metres occupied) *x* proportion of year for which training lasts	
Refreshments	Invoiced amount	
Equipment	Invoiced cost of hire or calculation based on annual depreciation or rental charge *x* proportion of year for which training lasts	
Materials	Cost of purchase or calculation based on length of time taken to produce	
Learners' time	Actual hourly rates or learners' average hourly rate of pay *x* number of hours devoted to training *x* number of learners	
Travel and out-of-pocket expenses	Expenses claimed + cost of any transport provided (including driver time for in-house staff)	
Books and exam fees	Invoiced cost	
	TOTAL	

pension contributions, etc), divide them by the number of working hours in the year to get a cost per working hour, and then multiply this by hours spent. That would, however, overlook the fact that there will be periods in the day/week/year when the trainer is not engaged on design, delivery or evaluation, but on other activities. These might include:

■ undergoing training themselves

■ developing materials for use in a variety of training

■ holidays

■ meetings

■ non-course-specific administration

■ being appraised

■ assisting colleagues.

To ensure that the full costs of operating the training function are taken into account, a standard charge-out rate is calculated. This can vary for each trainer to reflect actual salary and on-costs or be averaged across all the trainers. If there are no significant differences in their rates of pay and they are basically interchangeable, the latter will usually be sufficiently accurate. This approach has the advantage that the annual salaries and on-costs of managers, clerical and admin staff not directly involved in training can be added to give the total departmental salary costs. (Some organisations add the other departmental overhead costs, like office space and running costs, in to the calculation as well.)

To calculate the final charge-out rate, assumptions about trainer productivity have to be made. (This can be calculated more precisely by asking all trainers to keep a detailed log of how much time they spend on each activity, and using this as the basis of a productivity calculation. The sum of the hours spent on direct training activity – including pre-course discussion of training needs, training design, delivery and evaluation – can then be calculated as a percentage of the total hours available. The administrative burden this creates can be eased if the log is computerised.)

Depending on the level and complexity of the training offered and the way in which the department operates, it may be reasonable to assume that each trainer is working on chargeable activities for, say, 65 per cent of the working year. Assume that the total salary and on-costs for the department are £200,000, that there are five trainers, a manager and a part time administrator, and that there are 205 days in each trainer's working year – of which 65 per cent will be chargeable (133.25 days). The department will need to cover its total costs by spreading them over 666.25 days (five trainers @ 133.25 days each). This works out at £300 per trainer day (£200,000 divided by 666.25).

Organisations that adopt this sort of detailed costing approach tend to do so because the training budget is decentralised. If each part of the organisation has its own training budget, any centralised training function may have to operate as a profit centre. This means that it will charge other departments for its services and use the income to pay for the costs of employing staff and providing training. At the end of each financial year it is expected to make sure that its income at least covers its expenditure.

Such internal charging regimes

- help to focus attention on the real cost of each training activity
- encourage in-house training departments to be cost-effective in order to compete with external providers
- make individual heads of department accountable for their own expenditure. Because they are the people who are answerable for their results, there is some logic in saying they should be the ones who decide whether or not to go ahead with particular training
- create a significant additional administrative burden for the training department, which must keep track of all the time devoted to particular projects and make sure that it all gets charged out correctly
- create a significant additional burden for the accounts department, which must process these internal transactions to ensure that income and expenditure are allocated to the right profit centre.

The alternative is to accept the training function as a business overhead – part of the costs of running the organisation – and operate it as a cost centre. This means it can spend money up to the budget allocated to it, but does not have to generate revenue or make a profit.

When training operates in this way, the budget is usually centralised and held by the training manager. The annual training plan (see Chapter 2) is then costed out and broken down by departments. This is used to inform senior management of how it is intended to spend the money allocated. The budget will have to be sufficient to meet all the costs of running the department and delivering training. It does not usually include the learners' time or expenses unless they are classed as full-time trainees who may ultimately work anywhere in the organisation.

This approach

- reduces the amount of internal administration involved – although it is still important to keep an eye on both trainer productivity and overhead costs

- increases the visibility to senior management of the total spent on training. This can be a bad thing when times are hard and budgets are being cut

- recognises that training and developing employees should benefit the organisation as a whole. Why should the head of customer care meet the whole cost of training when the sales manager will benefit from increased revenue from more loyal customers?

The outcome of debates about the pros and cons of centralised versus decentralised budgets will depend on whether top management is convinced that they will get better value for their expenditure on training from allowing one person – probably the training manager – to oversee its allocation. Some organisations take the view that this is the best way of achieving the economies of scale which can come from centralisation. Others believe that a 'free market' approach, in which in-house training facilities compete for business with external sources, helps to safeguard quality and ensure value for money. There is no right answer, and many organisations have tried both approaches – some more than once!

Others operate a hybrid between the two approaches, allocating some funds on a decentralised basis to individual departments and centralising some to cover salaries and running costs for the training department. This can be a mixed blessing. It gives the training department the security of a cost-centre budget for fixed costs but can create tensions when individual departments decide to look elsewhere for training provision. This can mean poor use of resources for the organisation, leaving training department staff underemployed when other departments decline to use their services. The organisation's training policy (Chapter 1) can be written to prevent this, by insisting that internal resources are used wherever available – but this will not always be the best solution.

If you are responsible for managing all or part of a training budget, you will need to

- fight your corner in the annual budget round if you are a cost centre. You will need to make sure you are allocated enough money to cover the full cost of delivering the training plan

- make sure that the quality and availability of training delivered by the in-house team warrants other departments' paying for their services. If you are a profit centre, you will go out of business unless you do this. If you are not a profit centre, you will nevertheless be selling the organisation short by failing to pay sufficient attention to your competitive position

- make sure that all transactions get properly coded to the correct accounting code

- check spend against budget on a regular basis. Anticipate any shortfall or surplus and adapt your plans accordingly.

FUNDING TRAINING

At present, the lion's share of the cost of training the workforce is met by employers. It is estimated that, in England alone, organisations spend some £23 billion a year on training-related activity. The Learning and Skills Council's (LSC) public funding for all forms of adult learning was only about one tenth of that in its first year of operation (2001–02).

Apart from the Modern Apprenticeship programme described in Chapter 1, the main route by which employers are able to benefit from public funding is, as we saw in Chapter 3, through their employees taking part in LSC-funded courses at colleges of further education. Although fees are payable, much of the cost is met by the LSC. One disadvantage, for employers, has tended to be the requirement for whole qualifications to be studied – often entailing time away from the workplace.

The publication in 2003 of the government's strategy document *21st Century Skills, Realising our Potential,* paves the way for a rethink of the arrangements for funding the development of adult learning and skills. Under the proposals, from September 2005 all adults who do not already have a level 2 qualification (equivalent to five GCSE passes at grades A–C or an NVQ 2) will be entitled to free tuition to get one. This will extend the present priority of improving adults' basic literacy, language and numeracy skills to provide a subsidy for job-specific training at level 2. Where there are skill shortages in particular regions or employment sectors, the entitlement may extend to level 3 (equivalent to two 'A' levels or an NVQ 3.)

Since the amount of public money that can be devoted to education and training is inevitably limited, this may mean that the current levels of subsidy for employees attending other education courses, or who are already qualified beyond the relevant level, may have to be reduced. Advice for employers to help them access relevant and cost-effective training is set to improve, however, and the relevance and flexibility of publicly funded courses should increase following the planned reform of vocational qualifications for adults and the national roll-out of the Employer Training Pilots now taking place in 12 LSC areas.

Evaluation of these pilots should be completed by the end of 2005. The aim is to evaluate whether employers will be encouraged to train employees if they are subsidised for doing so. Different approaches and levels of subsidy are being tested among employers ranging in size from those with fewer than 50 employees to those with more than 250 staff. There is extra support for the smallest firms (those with fewer than 50 employees), and a contribution towards the cost of assessment, training and accreditation for employees who work towards recognised qualifications at NVQ level 2. Subsidies take the form of grants from the local LSC to meet the wage costs of staff taking time off to study.

It is therefore well worth opening a dialogue with your local LSC to establish whether and when training that you would like to do could be eligible for financial support. Particularly if the training will assist in the development of basic skills alongside other, more organisation-specific outcomes, you may well be eligible for some funding. You can locate your local LSC via the national LSC website www.lsc.gov.uk or the local telephone directory.

ADMINISTRATION AND RECORD-KEEPING
Training information

As a trainer, your credibility will be higher and your task immeasurably easier if you can provide

- clear, timely and accurate information for individual employees and their bosses, before, during and after training
- careful and relevant analysis of information as a basis for management decision-making – about individual employees, groups of employees and training overall.

The sort of questions you may be expected to answer fall into six broad categories:

- questions about training courses
- questions about training providers
- questions about individuals
- questions about groups of employees
- questions about policies and procedures
- questions about costs and benefits.

Questions about training courses

When is the next team leaders' course? What time does it start? Who else is on it? What are the travel arrangements? Will I be able to come back for a key meeting on the second morning? What do I need to bring with me? Is there an exam? Who do I tell about my special dietary requirements? When was the last time we redesigned the induction course? How long have we been running manual handling courses? How many people have been on them? What is the maximum number per course? Mark is on the Health and Safety course but I need to contact him urgently – how do I get hold of him? These and many more detailed questions will be directed at the course organiser or administrator on a regular basis. To answer them, a detailed course file is needed.

Questions about training providers

Where's the best place for Harry to get his Portuguese up to scratch before we send him over there? My people want to get back into the habit of learning – how relevant are the courses at the local college? We'd like to sponsor one of our people on an MBA – is the focus on international marketing stronger at Harvard or at London Business School? Are there any good videos or DVDs on time management? Are there any good books about transformational leadership? Does the course at UWE lead to a diploma or to a certificate? Will they give any credit for prior learning? XYZ consultancy keep sending me details of their seminars – have we sent anyone on them? Are they any good?

The breadth and scope of possible questions is enormous. To answer them at all you will need access to national or international training indexes or a comprehensive database. To answer them well, you will need to understand more precisely the training need to be met – see Chapter 3.

Questions about individuals

Has George done the coaching module? When did Casey do Part 2 of the Statistical Process Control course? Who was his tutor for his project? What was Katie's score in the administration test? When was Robin trained on the Control of Substances Hazardous to Health Regulations? What was John's time-keeping like during the interviewing course? When is Nadine scheduled to do her follow-up to the presentation skills course? Which of the training needs we identified at David's last appraisal have we still to find ways of meeting? Without a comprehensive delegate file you will not be able to respond.

Questions about groups of employees

How many of our managers have been trained in the equal opportunities policy? What proportion of the warehouse team are qualified to drive fork-lifts? How many of our shop floor are working towards NVQs? How many days' training did the machine shop get last year? Has everyone who operates a VDU had full training in the use of display screen equipment? How many of our team leaders need training in conflict resolution? How many new recruits receive training within one month of joining? Only by collating individual data for the relevant department or category of employee will you be able to answer these questions.

Questions about policies and procedures

Who do I have to get to authorise my enrolment for an Open University degree? How much exam leave am I entitled to? I can't spare Jennie on Wednesday afternoons, but she seems to think she's entitled to half-day release to do her accountancy course – who is right? My course tutor says we have to buy these three textbooks – but they'll cost £75 – who pays? The college have rung me to ask where Michael is. He's supposed to be there. Whose job is it to investigate and discipline him? Justine refuses to go on the residential leadership course we've nominated her for because she has no one to look after her children – can I force her to go?

Again the possible questions are many and varied. To answer them you will need to refer to your organisation's training policy and be prepared to search for examples of how similar cases have been handled in the past.

Questions about costs and benefits

How much did we spend, per employee, last year on training? Is that more or less than the year before? Which departments spend most on training – per employee, and overall? How many training course places were left unfilled this year? How many of our people have been promoted within six months of attending a personal development course? What proportion of our management trainees leave within 12 months of completing the programme? What value can we put on the changes we have made since we introduced the new 'design for innovation' course? How does that compare with the cost of the courses? What does it really cost us to put someone through the two-year technical training programme? Would it be cheaper to disband our central training team and rely on external providers? What is the correlation between the increases in our training expenditure over the last five years and the improvements in our return on sales?

Some of the information to answer questions like these may be drawn from the course and individual data mentioned above. As we have seen, accurate information about costs and benefits may be harder to get.

To be ready with answers

Anticipating the sort of questions that may be asked involves:

■ talking to line management, to establish what they feel they must know, under each of the six headings we have discussed. If resources permit, you can also invite them to identify what they would like to know on a regular basis

■ identifying the kind of questions that may come from outside the organisation. The Health and Safety Inspectorate, the Equal Opportunities Commission and the Commission for Racial Equality are just some of the official bodies that may ask for general information from time to time. An accident or complaint could trigger a specific enquiry

■ talking to other members of the training team to establish what questions they have been asked in the past, and to agree what sort of information you should be in a position to supply.

To help get started, set yourself up a log book or diary to record, each day, any requests for information which you have not been able to provide. If appropriate, see if you can persuade your colleagues to do the same. Review this once a month to see what light it sheds on the kind of information you should be keeping.

The extent to which you are able to meet every request will depend on the depth and breadth of the database you inherit or build. The speed with which you do so will depend on the human and/or computer-based resources you have.

Building the database will involve

■ source documents such as performance appraisal reports or training needs analyses

■ a standard pro forma for information about training events – to record objectives, duration, number of delegates, location, costs, and so forth, plus, after the event, attendance lists, delegate details and performance records

■ pro formas for evaluation of training to enable trainees and their managers to provide feedback

■ Internet search facilities or a library of training materials and course information.

As we shall see in the next section, a computerised database will reduce the need for paper forms by allowing authorised managers to update information directly. Line managers and/or individual employees can be trained to identify and record training needs as they arise. Those delivering training can be trained to input and amend information about training events as they occur.

It can be more difficult to keep track of employees themselves. James White may have been a team leader in the warehouse when his last training needs analysis form was completed. If he is now a supervisor in transport, you need some way of checking that this is the same James White, and that his training needs, activities and costs are recorded against the right department. The closer the links between the training and personnel information systems – see below – the less of a problem this is likely to be.

Setting up an information system

In all but the very smallest organisations, training administration is likely to involve using some sort of computer-based system. This should ideally be one which can be networked to individual trainers and perhaps line managers. By ensuring appropriate integration with the personnel/HR system, if there is one, it will be possible to keep track of employees' movements and costs without complex updating procedures.

If you are involved in choosing new hardware to run the training system, it is advisable to seek specialist advice. If you are buying or leasing new hardware, it could be worth thinking laterally about the other uses to which it could be put. Provided that it can be reconciled with the administrator's work schedule, a high-specification PC with Internet access, DVD and CD-ROM drives can serve multiple purposes, not just for the administrator. Even if it is only available at lunchtimes or in the evenings, it could enable you to provide additional training for those who need it (see Chapter 4).

If you are involved in choosing software, you must be clear whether you need

- a means of storing and retrieving individual items of information – ie a straight alternative to a card index

or
- a means of re-sorting and analysing data – by course, by department, by date, by employee category, and so on.

If it is the latter, you will need a training database of some sort, either developed internally or selected from the proprietary systems now available.

The most sophisticated of these will not only re-cut and analyse your data but present it for you graphically so you can monitor trends – in costs, numbers, performance ratings, achievement of course objectives – over time. They can also assist in planning future training by enabling you to model 'what-if' scenarios. What will it cost if everyone who needs project management skills goes on a three-day external course? What if we use a four-day internal one instead? What if we can only afford to respond to training needs classified as top-priority? What will it cost? What needs will we fail to meet?

Even if you cannot afford or do not need this level of sophistication, you will almost certainly want your system to be capable of producing routine documentation like course invitations, joining instructions, delegate lists, requests for pre- and post-course work and evaluation. The technology is now widely available to enable you to do all these things automatically, once course and delegate details are entered.

Sources of information

The efficient administration of training depends on the accuracy and timeliness of information flow. Mistakes, in joining instructions, course bookings, follow-up or the recording of information, can be costly and damage the reputation of the training function. The more comprehensive and up-to-date the training database, the less this is likely to be a problem. If you are charged with setting up such a system, do seek specialist advice.

Establishing a database

Computer manufacturers and software houses will be happy to tell you about their products and advise on their use. If there is already a personnel or HR administration system in place and working effectively, find out about any training add-ons that may be available.

Other employers may be prepared to give you the benefit of their experience, so always ask potential system suppliers to give you the names of other users. Talk to them and, if possible, visit them to see the system in action. The picture they paint will sometimes be rather different from the one the supplier has tried to create.

Guidance on administration

Short courses designed for those new to training administration are offered regularly by the Chartered Institute of Personnel and Development (CIPD).

Information about training providers

Course objectives, target audiences, costs, venues, dates and some indication of effectiveness can be obtained most readily over the Internet. For many trainers this has now largely superseded paper-based directories. You will need an appropriate search engine and the skills to use it to narrow down your search. Alternatively, the *learndirect* helpline mentioned in Chapter 3 is there to assist, while your local LSC should have a database of the local providers that it funds.

SUMMARY: QUICK TIPS

- The first step in setting up a specialist training function is to be absolutely clear about the nature of your role and the resources available to you.

- Clarify whether the department is to operate as a profit centre, selling its services to other department, or a cost centre, funded from central organisational resources.

- To perform effectively, you will need information to enable you to answer questions – about courses, training providers, individuals and groups of learners, policies and procedures, costs and benefits. To answer them, you will need, as a minimum:
  - individual records – to include information about training needs, training received, results attained
  - course files – to record objectives, duration, location, attendees, costs, results
  - a training index – to identify potential providers, dates, location and costs

- By working closely with line managers and other members of the training team you should get a feel for the sort of internal questions which may arise. To enable you to respond to enquiries from official external bodies, the safest course is to establish a relationship with local representatives.

- A computerised database will speed up the collation and analysis of data – but must be registered with the Data Protection Registrar (see Chapter 1).

The trainer today and tomorrow

CURRENT ISSUES IN TRAINING

The operational issues that will face you as a trainer are many and varied. In this section our focus is at a more strategic level and has to do with the developing role of the training within the wider organisation. We single out four aspects:

- creating a learning organisation
- optimising e-learning
- the trainer as coach versus the trainer as instructor
- the trainer as performance improvement consultant.

Creating a learning organisation

Some organisations stagger blindly from one crisis to the next, never pausing to draw out the lessons from one disaster before the next is upon it. Others consciously plan for and cope with change, and learn continuously from it. Those in the second category characterise what is meant by the phrase 'learning organisation'.

Such an organisation constantly seeks out and finds ways of sharing and using all the thinking capability, expertise and knowledge accumulated by its employees. It may also draw on its supply chain and other contacts, to further enhance its store of learning

Becoming a learning organisation is not something that happens by accident. It happens as a result of a conscious, strategic decision to create the kind of culture that supports learning, and to put in place the processes that will enable it to happen. There is no one formula but a number of well-publicised variations on the same theme.

In Chapter 2 we touched on the link between training and business planning. In a learning organisation, business plans are about learning. The chief executive, or other very senior champion, sees learning as being as much a part of what the organisation is about as the products it creates or the money it makes. Management style, performance management and reward systems (see Chapter 1) are all geared to encouraging learning rather than maintaining the status quo.

The precise forms of learning that are embraced by learning organisations vary. Most include a significant element of self-development, encouraged by the provision of diagnostic tools, opportunities to work with others who share the same objectives in a learning set or group, and ready access to technology-based and other learning resources. David Megginson and Vivien Whitaker describe how this works in practice in *Cultivating Self-development*.

Team learning, to enable those who work together to plan and learn together, is another important facet of the learning organisation. This recognises that the whole is usually greater than the sum of the parts and that teams who have shared goals, common experiences and mutual understanding are stronger than collections of individuals, however bright.

Over and above this, the learning organisation has in place the means of sharing learning across the business. This may take many forms, from formal feedback sessions from individuals who have attended external training events to the development of databases of best practice and expertise. Particularly in large, decentralised organisations, networking – whether by computer or in person – is crucial in preventing wheels which have already been invented by one team being reinvented by others.

Optimising e-learning

There are two main schools of thought about the emerging role of electronic learning via the Internet and the World-Wide Web (e-learning).

- The web is an alternative classroom in which presentations, practice and tests are done on line, but with the limitations that
  - much of the material available on the web is generic and therefore not applicable to specific organisations or situations. This therefore has some of the same drawbacks as the public/open training courses reviewed in Chapter 3
  - much of the material is knowledge, rather than skills-, attitude- or competence-based. E-learning does not seem to work effectively for coaching, skills practice or interpersonal interaction
  - from time to time individuals and organisations experience difficulties with the reliability and speed of the technology and access to it
  - while some learners cope self-sufficiently with the medium and the content, others need more support with one or both and may fall prey to some of the disadvantages of distance learning identified in Chapter 3.

  Some of these difficulties are being overcome by organisations customising material for their own employees to increase their relevance. Training in in-store systems at B&Q, for instance, is increasingly web-based. Some NHS Trusts have developed material specific to the treatment of particular conditions, and the Crown Prosecution Service has developed e-learning on the treatment of vulnerable witnesses.

- The web provides a framework within which technology acts as a coach and consultant to guide decision-making at critical points. Allison Rossett in *The ASTD e-learning Handbook: Best practices, strategies and case studies for an emerging field* identifies five separate functions of what she calls the 'big tent' of e-learning:
  - learning in the traditional sense – which enables courses to be downloaded at home or in the

workplace and to be supported by a tutor, either on line or in person at a local centre. Such facilities are now available in the UK via the Ufl/*learndirect* network of local centres. Contact www.learndirect.co.uk

- information wrap-around – which provides a body of materials that enable someone to act intelligently and quickly in a given situation. This might include checklists for trouble-shooting or samples of particular tasks. The teaching resources on the website www.kn.pacbell.com provide examples
- interaction and collaboration – which is where the technology engages and connects people with others who share their interests and/or who are working on similar tasks, via online open discussion
- performance support – which provides online guidance to enable individuals to perform as if they know more than they do. E-learning can provide active support by tailoring the information it gives to suit inputs that the learner provides. For instance, technology can enable an emergency service operator to give detailed instructions on how to deal with a casualty – not because he or she is a fully trained doctor but because the system responds to information about the condition of the patient
- guidance and tracking: some on-line technology provides a clear picture of the standard of performance that is expected and can guide the user towards developing critical skills he or she does not currently have.

There is an increasing number of websites that can provide an insight into how e-learning is currently developing. You can visit www.learndirect-business.co.uk for some British examples.

Whichever way technology develops, it is unlikely that it will provide a complete substitute for the human trainer any time soon. And the role of the trainer continues to develop in other directions too. In particular,

The trainer as coach versus the trainer as instructor

As we saw in Chapter 1, the role of the trainer varies from organisation to organisation. One common thread which does seem to have emerged in recent years is the move

- away from didactic, classroom-based instruction in 'how to do it' (whether 'it' is threading a sewing machine or managing a department)
- towards much more emphasis on coaching to allow the learner to take responsibility and, with support and guidance, work out how 'it' works best for them. We explored this in Chapter 6.

Alongside this evolution in training styles, there has been an equally fundamental shift in training roles. As organisations become more complex and the pace of change gets faster, few can really pretend they know all the answers. Instead of trying to be ready with the solution to every problem, trainers have learnt what perhaps they always knew. By holding a mirror up to the questioner you can often find a better and more workable solution than proposing something from outside.

Management consultants have known this for years. There is an unkind saying that a consultant will 'borrow your watch and then tell you the time'. What it means is that outsiders rarely have an instant recipe to transform an organisation. Instead, what they do is help managers see the weaknesses in their present approach and identify some of the options they might choose to improve matters. Whether they do choose – and then whether they do everything necessary to make the chosen option work – is up to them.

This, increasingly, is what the trainer is attempting to do for the line manager. As line managers' own responsibility for the development of their people has become clearer and more widely accepted, they have become less ready to offload that responsibility onto a faceless collection of 'trainers' – whether internal or external.

The more interested managers are in helping their people to excel, the more they will look to the trainer to ask them the questions that will enable them to focus on

- what they want their people to be able to do
- what resources are available, from within the team and elsewhere
- how they will know when they have achieved their goal.

In that context, what the line manager needs is someone who can, in turn, *coach* him or her. Someone who will help identify and review alternatives – rather than someone who will provide the answers. This is a role many trainers are now adopting.

The trainer as performance improvement consultant

'Performance improvement consultant' is a label some professional trainers like to use. It implies that supporting self-development and linking it to the achievement of improved organisational performance is the way forward. The consultant's focus is on forming and nurturing partnerships with line managers in order to help them appreciate the wider implications of improving performance.

In this context, options and solutions well beyond the scope of the conventional training plan must be embraced. The whole range of personnel policy and practice – from recruitment and reward to communications and career planning – comes into play. Organisational structures and the design of business processes are as much part of the performance improvement consultant's thinking as the choice of learning methods or the design of training programmes. Project management and the management of change take over from course management and presentation as their key skills.

Underpinning the work of the performance improvement consultant is an understanding of the techniques and approaches associated with *business transformation*. This entails a fundamental re-think of the way the organisation works.

A whole raft of techniques can be brought to bear to make sure that every one of the processes in an organisation is as effective and as efficient as possible. These include:

- flowcharting and systematic problem-solving
- control charts
- pareto and other statistical techniques.

Information about what they involve and how to use them is to be found in Tom Boydell and Malcolm Leary's *Identifying Training Needs*.

The main steps in the process are listed below.

Elements of transformation

- Look critically at the *vision* and *mission* of the organisation.
- Identify the *critical success factors* or things which must be achieved if the vision and mission are to be attained.

- Define which *processes* are central to the critical success factors – and what each is intended to achieve.
- Understand exactly how each core process works, using flowcharts or *models* to capture the key activities and roles and responsibilities involved.
- Take detailed and repeated *measurements* to establish what each process is currently delivering, and identify where and why delays and errors occur.
- Use *systematic problem-solving techniques* to tackle the causes of failure.
- *Redesign* the processes to avoid unnecessary inspection, movement, delays and duplication.
- Build in *fail-safes* to prevent errors and defects.
- Redefine *roles and responsibilities* and train people to use the revised processes.
- Put *new measures* in place and monitor performance.

Tasks for the performance improvement consultant will include

- advising on the speed and direction of process improvement or transformation projects and encouraging prompt and effective decision-making at key points
- acting as team facilitator, coaching cross-functional teams and their leaders in the use of the diagnostic, problem-solving, measurement and decision-making tools appropriate at each stage
- helping the teams to identify individual and team training needs and ways of using the resources of the team to meet them. People who have been used to working as individuals do not always adjust immediately to become effective teamworkers. Those skilled in team-building can find themselves much in demand as new teams form and try to get established
- documenting and recording new processes so that the team will not to revert to the old way of doing things.

THE TRAINER'S PERSON SPECIFICATION

The exact requirements of the trainer of the future will depend on the industry, the employer, and the level and nature of the role. In some, administration and record-keeping will continue to have a high profile. In others, interpersonal and coaching skills will be critical. In yet others, the ability to develop customised e-learning tools will be more important.

As we have seen, the emphasis is likely to be on helping people – and organisations – to learn, rather than on traditional trainer input.

The checklist in Table 28 should be seen as a list of possibilities rather than a definitive prescription.

BUILDING RELATIONSHIPS

The relationship between trainer and learner is an important one in any training situation. As we saw in the first section of Chapter 6, difficulties here can act as real barriers to learning. Beyond this, the trainer often needs to build a relationship with learners' line managers, not only to fulfil the sort of roles outlined earlier in this chapter but also for the identification of needs and the evaluation of outcomes.

The skills of *negotiating*, *influencing* and *persuading* are likely to be essential to your credibility as a trainer. Without them, you will be unable to promote your ideas, influence others and sell necessary changes. So alongside the tools and techniques of coaching, questioning and listening (Chapter 6) and of interviewing (Chapter 2), you should consider how best to develop these skills.

Table 28   *Trainer skills*

Skill(s) or competence(s)	Application
Interpersonal skills	to establish rapport at all levels: questioning, listening and summarising are key
Negotiating and persuading skills	to make sure that others understand the value of training
Sensitivity	to pick up how learners and their managers are responding to training
Assertiveness	to ensure that the importance of training is not overlooked
Empathy	to identify with where learners are starting from and what they are experiencing
Communication skills	to convey new and challenging ideas clearly, logically and succinctly
Creative skills	to design imaginative approaches to training design and delivery
Analytical and evaluative skills	for interpreting behaviour and information – including financial and other numerical data
Time management skills	to make effective use of time, inside and outside the training room
Administrative skills	to ensure that training is planned, recorded and monitored effectively
Commercial awareness	to ensure that training resources are used cost-effectively and, in some instances, profitably – to serve the needs of the business
Technical skills	to operate computer systems and, possibly, develop technology-based training modules
Personal credibility	as someone who knows about and can add value to the learning process
Wide knowledge and understanding of the organisation, its goals, values and processes	to contribute to the re-engineering of business processes and to develop learning which is consistent with corporate goals and values
Integrity	to safeguard the confidentiality of information: trainers are increasingly involved in sensitive personal and business issues
Respect for authority	to help establish the norms of the organisation – you need to be accepted as part of its management team
Tolerance of ambiguity	as organisations and individuals struggle with new learning challenges, trainers will often find themselves pulled in conflicting directions

Negotiating

Negotiating is a particular form of interaction between two or more people or groups. It implies that those involved have different ideas – either about the desired outcome of the meeting or about how it should be reached. Often used to describe the interchanges that take place between management and trade unions over matters such as pay and conditions, the process applies wherever there are differences of view to be reconciled.

Negotiations do not have to result in win/lose outcomes, in which one party achieves its objective and the other party loses out completely. They achieve most when they lead to win/win. Martin and Jackson in *Personnel Practice* use the example of a negotiation over an orange which two people want. There are several ways in which the negotiation could end.

- One keeps the orange – he wins, she loses.
- The other keeps the orange – she wins, he loses.
- They cut the orange in half – a compromise by which both surrender something and gain something although it is not what either might most have wanted.
- They divide the orange so that one keeps the peel for the purpose she required and the other keeps the fruit for his own purposes.

This last outcome is a truly collaborative win/win, in which both sides achieve their primary objective without detriment to the other.

A range of factors will influence the outcome of any negotiation. In particular, you will need:

- clear objectives – the outcome you really want to reach, and any subsidiary goals that you are prepared to surrender along the way
- recognition of the other party's point of view
- research – into the facts which support any claims you or the other party may wish to make
- rehearsal – to think through various routes the negotiation may follow – and what you will do if it does. Some of the behaviours you will find helpful are:

  - Keep your own key objectives clearly in mind. If you are more interested in the outcome than the process, be prepared to concede ground on the latter.
  - Ask questions to clarify exactly what the other party would like to get out of the dialogue, as well as where the other party currently stands in relation to the issue (the guidance on questioning in Chapter 6 will help).
  - Agree whether you have a finite time-limit for the discussion or will stay until agreement has been reached. If you can be flexible about this – without making it look as though you have all the time in the world – it will put some subtle pressure on the other party.
  - Listen carefully – and let the other party know that you are taking their point of view seriously by nodding and using positive body language. If you sit with your arms crossed looking defensive, or lean forward poking your finger at them, you may find you have raised the temperature of the debate unhelpfully without saying a word.
  - Show you understand. Try 'mirroring' the other party's position in subtle ways to let them know you can see it their way. If, for instance, they are sitting with their hands tightly clasped, clasp yours too and then gradually shift to a more relaxed position to help ease the tension.
  - Keep cool. Even if the other party's case seems weak or silly to you, do not let them see that that is your opinion. Keep asking questions about, in particular, what they think the

consequences might be – for the organisation, for other people, for the learner or the learning, of doing things as they suggest.

- Constantly look for alternative ways to achieve your objective. 'What if?' is a very useful gambit.
- Summarise regularly to capture points of agreement and to highlight areas where you still see things differently.
- If you are going round in circles or seem to have got locked into a dead-end debate, suggest you both go away to reflect on the discussion so far and reconvene later.
- Once you have reached agreement, summarise it and volunteer to draft a note setting out the main conclusions reached. Do it promptly and send it to the other party asking for comment on any omissions or misrepresentation. Make any minor amendments they suggest if these do not invalidate the agreement reached.

Assertiveness

Being assertive is critical to effective persuasion and negotiation. Ken and Kate Back in *Assertiveness Training for Meetings* distinguish between 'assertive', 'submissive' and 'aggressive' behaviour. The characteristics of each are set out in Table 29.

Table 29   *Styles of interpersonal behaviour*

Aggressive	Assertive	Submissive
I have little respect for others.	I respect others and myself.	I feel inferior to others.
I believe I'm OK and the other person isn't – I seek to dominate and put my own needs and ideas first.	I believe we're both OK. I am direct and honest and think others' needs and ideas are as important as mine.	I believe the other person is OK and I'm not. I let other people put their needs and ideas first
I tend to speak loudly and blame and challenge others. I can be sarcastic.	I speak clearly and audibly with a tone which is steady and clear.	I tend to speak quietly and may swallow my words. I often sound nervous or apologetic.
I tend to adopt a hostile stance with arms folded or behind my head or with my fingertips pressed together to show my superiority.	I look people in the eye, use open hand movements and keep my arms open or lightly crossed.	I tend to keep my eyes down and my shoulders hunched and sometimes cover my mouth with my hand or make nervous hand movements.
I use 'I' a lot and boast about things I have done; I express my opinions as if they were facts.	I make clear unqualified statements to put forward my views. I don't pass my opinions off as facts.	I qualify my opinions with lots of 'maybe' words and put myself down or distance myself from my own ideas.
I relish conflict and like to keep disagreements going.	I acknowledge conflict and address it, looking for ways to move on.	I avoid direct conflict wherever possible.

WRITING REPORTS

As a trainer, you may need to produce reports on a number of topics, including

- individual learners
- specific training programmes
- the development of the training function.

Whatever the type of the report, start by making sure you that you understand the objective. This may be to inform or persuade, to describe or to analyse, and whichever it is will affect the tone, style and content of what you write. Particular aspects to consider to make sure that your report achieves the impact and the outcome you want, and that it adds to your credibility in the organisation, are:

- layout
- presentation
- structure.

Layout

This should be kept clear and unfussy. If there is a standard corporate style and layout in use in your organisation, use that. If not, choose a clear type-face like Times New Roman or Garamond. Use **bold** type for headings and (sparingly) to add emphasis. Make sure that the directory/folder/file name/date appears unobtrusively on each page, and that page numbers are inserted. Check all page numbers, headings and cross-references as part of a final proofcheck. Adopt and stick to a simple framework of paragraph numbering. Use short sentences, paragraphs and bullet points to break up the text.

Presentation

Use good-quality paper and make sure that the reprographic process does not leave it looking smudged, crooked or dirty. If the report is only a few pages long, a staple will suffice to hold it together. For longer reports and those which are likely to be circulated around the organisation and/or have a life-span of more than a week or two, a cover and more secure slide or clip binding will prevent it from getting too tatty too quickly.

Structure

This is vital if you are to lead the reader through to a logical conclusion and some recommendations that are likely to be accepted by your intended audience. It should include:

Title page	The title should reflect the subject matter and purpose of the report – eg *A proposal to enhance the effectiveness of team training in ABC Company*. The author's name and position plus the date, corporate logo and any requirements regarding confidentiality or restriction of circulation should also appear on the front page.
Executive summary	If the report extends to more than a few pages, busy readers may not even look at it unless there is something quick and easy to help them decide whether to devote any time to the report. The executive summary should provide a brief synopsis of the content of the report, focusing on the main conclusions and recommendations. The reader who wants to understand the chapter and verse that support your argument will study the full report, but the executive summary must be persuasive because it may be all that some of the audience look at.

Acknowledgements	In a business report these should be kept to minimum. If you single out some managers and not others, you risk upsetting those you didn't name; if you start describing how grateful you are to all the organisations you have visited or bodies you have contacted, it may antagonise readers who want to get to the facts as quickly as possible. Just list them briefly. If you want the audience to know how helpful your auntie was in proofreading the report, find some other way of telling them.
Contents page	You should draft this before you start writing the report, to give you a framework, but revisit it afterwards to make sure it still reflects the content and the sequence you actually followed, and to add page numbers. Most reports will need the sections identified in this list, with a further breakdown of the major ones if they extend to more than a couple of pages each.
Terms of reference	These clarify the subject matter of the report (eg *an evaluation of the team-building programme*), the reason for it (eg *as part of the on-going programme of review and evaluation of training*), and the audience for whom it is intended (eg *senior managers*).
Aim	This sets out what you want to happen as an outcome of the report – eg *to enable management to determine whether and when the programme should be repeated.*
Objectives	These break the aim down into greater detail – eg (i) *to explain the objectives of the team-building programme, what it entailed, and who attended* (ii) *to describe the process of post-course evaluation* (iii) *to review changes in the job performance of those who attended* (iv) *to identify any other factors apart from the programme which could account for changes in performance* (v) *to define criteria against which alternative means of achieving the same objective should be judged and apply these to a range of possible alternatives* (vi) *to outline a proposal for a repeat of the programme, with modifications to reflect the outcome of the evaluation.*
Introduction	This should provide a brief background to the requirement for the report and information to help orientate the reader – eg *The team-building programme was originally started in September 1998 and was last reviewed in August 2001. It has been running in its present form since February 2002. Since its inception . . .* (Numbers of participants, major changes in content, etc may warrant a mention, as may a brief account of the training department's commitment to review and evaluation.)
Methodology	This describes how the task of researching and writing the report has been approached – eg *a review of the course documentation and delegates' reactions-level evaluations, structured interview with the consultant who ran the programme, analysis of pre- and post-course appraisal reports, use of a specially designed follow-up report the completion of which was discussed with participants and their line managers, a review of articles in professional journals to identify alternative approaches, etc.*
Main body	This presents the facts and data as they relate to the aims of the report. It may be partly descriptive, identifying what the review process revealed. It should also include some analysis to quantify your observations and pull out the implications. In our example, you might include some tables or graphs showing how performance has developed against key measures for particular individuals, or how many of the evaluations reported positive, negative or intermediate responses. It would also be relevant to include some discussion of the criteria against which the effectiveness of the training has been evaluated. Subsections should be used for each new topic, and it should be clear to the reader how these relate to the aims.

Conclusions	This is where you put forward your view of what the data are telling you, and must follow from the information contained in the body of the report. If the report had several interconnected aims, as in our example, you may want to itemise the conclusions and group them according to the aim to which they relate. Conclusions should be clear and succinct, and must follow from the facts presented in the body of the report – eg *Those participants who had a detailed pre-course discussion with their line manager about the objectives they hoped to achieve on the course were more likely afterwards to show positive changes in performance.*
Options	There are likely to be a number of ways of responding to the conclusions you have drawn. This section should explain what these are – even the ones you think are not particularly attractive. The criteria for choosing between options should be spelled out, and the pros and cons of each discussed in the light of these. Tabular formats, rather than rambling debates, are likely to be most compelling.
Recommendations	These should follow logically from the analysis of the conclusions and be clear and action-oriented – eg *Line managers should be issued with materials to help them conduct a formal briefing session before participants attend. ACTION: training officer.*
Appendices	Rather than cluttering the report with long descriptions or detailed source data, these can be put in separately numbered appendices at the end of the report. Reference can then be made in the text without interrupting the flow of the argument – eg *For full details of delegates and dates attended, see Appendix 1.*
References	If you have consulted texts and journals, these should be referred to in the text with full details given in the Appendix. The correct form is for textual references to include just the author's name and the date. The reference listing can then give full details, as in the *Further reading* section of this book.

MANAGING YOUR TIME

To be effective as a trainer (or in most other roles, for that matter), you will need to make best use of your working day. Some people seem to be able to be able to achieve more in each day than others, not because they are cleverer or do things quicker but because they are good at managing their time. Good time management has many benefits including

- higher productivity – you get more done and your organisation gets better value for its investment in you
- less stress – you feel more in control and are under less pressure
- more effective decision-making – because key tasks have more time devoted to them and are approached in a more organised manner
- fewer errors – for the same reason.

The essence of good time management is not the latest palm-held organiser or a leather-bound *Time-manager* diary. It is clarity of purpose and priorities. If you focus on what you want to achieve – in any given year, month, week, day or hour – you will find it much easier to decide which tasks do need doing, which can wait, which can be passed to someone else or delegated, and which warrant no time spent on them at all.

The opposite of this approach is the 'busy fool' syndrome. It is possible to get so involved in doing things that you simply cannot see the wood for the trees. Sometimes this is a result of spending too much time

doing the easy tasks or the ones you enjoy while putting off those that will take longer or be more challenging.

To make the best use of your time, constant vigilance and a high level of awareness are required. The list
below highlights some of the things that will 'steal' time from you if you let them, together with some Do's
and Don'ts for dealing with them.

To schedule work effectively,

DO:
- Use a manual or electronic organiser to list the tasks you have to do (your 'to-do list'). Find ways
  of organising this that work for you. Dividing the tasks into those that are important and those
  that are urgent and marking them with flags or asterisks can help you focus on the ones that
  really matter – the ones that are urgent *and* important. Tick them off as you do them so you
  know that you are making progress.
- Schedule time into your diary for planning and reviewing your task lists and for work on major
  projects. The latter should be broken down into smaller tasks or phases of work in a realistic
  project plan. Set your own deadlines realistically in the light of how long particular tasks are
  likely to take. Tasks involving obtaining input or decisions from other people always take longer
  than you bargain for. Build in a time allowance in case the person whose authorisation you need
  at a critical point is away from the office. Better still, check out the person's movements and
  book a time in his or her diary for him or her to provide the input you need.

DON'T:
- Assume you will be able to 'just fit it in' if it is a major job. Any individual task that will take more
  than a few minutes to do deserves its own space in your diary.

To keep paper-work under control,

DO:
- Tackle one thing at a time. Picking things up and putting them down again all takes time. Aim
  to handle each piece of paper once only – use the RAFT system (Refer, Action, File, Throw
  away). Be ruthless: don't spend hours reading documents of marginal relevance – skim-read or
  look at the summary to see if you really need to read them. Have a simple filing system and
  use it, keeping documents in a consistent order (probably chronological) so you know where to
  look for things and thinning out occasionally to prevent them from becoming unwieldy.
- Use e-mail instead of a phonecall if it will save you having to write notes afterwards. Use voice-
  mail messages if you cannot get through to people only if you want to be interrupted by their
  return call. Otherwise, use the ring-back facility which you can ignore if you are busy on other
  things by the time they are free. Remember to call again later – and to set aside time for dealing with your own e-mail and voice-mail messages.

DON'T:
- Let paperwork pile up on your desk. You may worry that 'out of sight' will be 'out of mind' if you
  put it away, but a good 'to-do list' can ensure that you do not lose track of outstanding work,
  and the fewer papers you have lying around, the more efficient you will feel, the less time you
  will spend hunting for things under the debris, and the more businesslike other people will think
  you are.

To increase the effectiveness of meetings,

DO:

- Agree in advance how long a meeting is to last and what the objective is. If there is more than one objective, a timed agenda can keep people focused on which are the items that require most discussion. Meet in other people's offices so that you are able to get up and leave if you have more important things to do. If the chair is not making it clear what the purpose of each agenda item is – to decide, to air the options so that someone else can decide, to note a decision that has already been made or action that has already been taken – take the initiative and ask. Too many meetings develop a life of their own just because no one is assertive enough to say 'What is it *for*?'
- If you are in the chair, introduce each item by drawing attention to its nature and the time allotted to it. If someone is inclined to ramble on, interrupt politely to see if the others feel they are on course to reach the required outcome or would like some further work done outside the meeting first.

DON'T:

- Let people get too comfortable. Particularly if they have 'just dropped in', conduct the meeting standing up. Once you sit down, they may too, so be careful of signalling that you are prepared to settle into a longer discussion. And do not table any document longer than half of one side of A4 during a meeting. Issue it beforehand to allow other people the chance to digest it properly. That way, you are less likely to waste time in debate which could have been avoided if only the others had read it first.

To reduce the number of interruptions,

DO:

- Schedule 'surgery times' for those who need to see you. Make sure everyone knows when they are. Even if they do not use them, you can still legitimately turn them away at other times by drawing attention to the surgery hours. If possible, arrange for someone else to intercept your phonecalls if you need to work uninterrupted, but make sure they can do more than just promise that you will call back. If they can't, you might as well re-record your voice-mail message to say at what time you expect to return today's calls. Identify who else they can speak to if their call is urgent. And make sure you allow yourself enough time to return all calls.

DON'T:

- Get into the habit of interrupting others, or they may think they are simply returning the favour by interrupting you.

To make sure you feel in control,

DO:

- Work systematically. Decide whether you prefer to overhaul and add to your to-do list before you go home at night or first thing in the morning. Keep contact phone numbers, faxes and e-mail addresses ready to hand either on your system or in an indexed book. Always have a pad by the phone so you can take down messages. A hard-backed notebook which you can use as a 'day book' to keep notes of things as they happen works for some people and makes it easier to check back on any particular event.

DON'T:

■ Let it get on top of you. Take a break, even if it's only for a few minutes to fetch a coffee. Sometimes that is all it takes to get things back into perspective. And don't let the quest for perfection take over. Checking and re-checking your own and other people's work usually proves the law of diminishing returns. Know when it is at an acceptable standard – and let it go.

DEVELOPING YOUR SKILLS

The Chartered Institute of Personnel and Development (CIPD)

In order to develop a career in training, membership of the relevant professional body – the CIPD – is a distinct advantage. The Institute has an active programme of research into personnel/HR and training issues and provides short courses, conferences, in-company training solutions and a comprehensive library and information service. A national network of branches enables members to exchange good practice and keep up to date with developments in the field. There is a choice of membership routes which is kept under close review.

A network of CIPD centres offer a range of full-time, part time and/or flexible learning courses, aimed at people with all levels of experience from novices to senior practitioners. The qualifications include:

■ Certificate in Personnel Practice (CPP)

■ Certificate in Training Practice (CTP)

■ Certificate in Recruitment and Selection (CRS)

■ Professional Development Scheme (PDS).

Membership of the Institute is available at several levels, as shown in Table 30. From October 2003, Members, Fellows and Companions will be able to add the word 'Chartered' before the designation.

Table 30 *CIPD membership grades and criteria*

Level	Grade	Criteria
Full membership	Companion (CCIPD)	By invitation only
	Fellow (FCIPD)	Graduate member with ten years' relevant management experience plus CPD
	Member (MCIPD)	Graduate member with three years' management experience plus CPD
Other membership grades	Graduate	Successful completion of the PDS
	Licentiate	Part completion of the PDS
	Associate	Successful completion of one of the support-level certificates (eg CTP)
	Affiliate (studying and non-studying)	Open to all

There are five possible routes into membership:

■ *educational*   through a CIPD-approved course of study
■ *competence assessment*   against NVQ/SVQ standards

- *professional assessment*   against CIPD standards
- *accreditation of prior certificated*   through an approved CIPD alternative post-graduate-
  learning   level qualification and examination
- *a combination of the above*

For those new to training, the CTP provides both an introduction to training skills and a possible step towards professional membership. The course is available at colleges of further education and through other centres nationwide. This will help to equip you to embark on the graduate programme, which covers all aspects of personnel and development, but you should consult your course tutor or the CIPD Membership and Education Department about the differing demands of this higher-level programme.

The Institute has a policy of *continuing professional development* (CPD) which emphasises each individual's responsibility for his or her own learning. There are three main requirements:

- Members are expected to plan their learning and keep a record of it.
- Evidence of CPD must be provided to support applications to upgrade membership.
- All corporate members are required to undertake CPD and may be asked to participate in random surveys.

A wide range of different activities can contribute towards CPD – from attendance at branch events, seminars and conferences to self-development activities, coaching and mentoring. Whereas some professional bodies insist on specifying a set number of hours or attendance at specific training events, the CIPD has chosen to rely on its members to structure development to meet personal needs, recording the outcomes in a personal learning log. A CPD pack, including a CD-Rom for charting and planning development are available and there is an online facility.

For further information about CPD, and for details of both the professional education scheme and the programme of short courses offered by the Institute, you can contact the CIPD at

     CIPD House
     Camp Road
     London
     SW19 4UX
     Telephone: 020 8971 9000
     Fax: 020 8263 3333
     or via their website: www.cipd.co.uk/membership

Career paths in training

Few people enter the training function directly without spending part of their career in other functions first. This makes sense for most people, because the trainer whose awareness of the reality beyond the training room is limited may find it harder to empathise with learners and harder to plan and deliver training that is really relevant to them. Once in the function, there are three main career strands:

- training administration
- up-front training
- training management.

Although it is possible to move through from one strand to another, it is also quite common for training managers to move into the function after managerial experience elsewhere, and for up-front trainers to develop their careers laterally, by adding new areas of expertise, or vertically, by dealing with more senior people and getting involved in some of the coaching and internal consultancy roles described earlier in this chapter.

There is therefore no single career pathway. Indeed, many organisations recognise that personal and interpersonal skills can be developed during a spell in the training function as well as wider insight into the work of the organisation. They therefore actively encourage a period in training as part of a broader approach to career development.

Whether your stay in the training function is to be long or short, you will get the best from it if you:

- take responsibility for your own development
- set yourself long-term goals and constantly monitor your progress towards them. Wherever possible, these should be Specific, Measurable, Attainable, Relevant and Time-bounded (SMART). They may include specific competences you want to increase – skill in using web-based materials, for instance, or confidence in dealing assertively with senior managers – or other specific behaviours you would like to develop. Think what standards you want to reach, and how you will know when you have got there
- consider where and how else you can learn to meet your goals. You may need some off-the-job training yourself, or you may be able to achieve a lot on-the-job by always using the Plan–Do–Review model of operation to
- become a reflective practitioner – taking every opportunity to move yourself around the learning cycle after each training session you conduct or activity in which you get involved. Set up a diary or log book in which, after each major event you:
  - describe the experience and your part in it
  - note your observations about what you did and felt, what others did and what happened
  - review relevant theories or concepts that you brought, or could have brought, into play
  - reflect on
    - the objectives you hoped to achieve and how they fit with your long-term goals
    - the things you did that contributed positively towards achieving them
    - the things you did that detracted from achieving them
    - the things you could do differently next time
    - the expectation you have of the effect of such a change
  - plan to build the learning from this event into the way you operate in future:
    - What will you do?
    - When?
    - What barriers do you foresee?
    - What help will you need to overcome them?
    - How will you gauge your progress?
    - How will you know when you have succeeded?
- coach yourself wherever you can, using the approach outlined in Chapter 6. Where you feel it would be helpful, involve a colleague or your manager.

Remember: the job of the trainer is about learning – *make sure that that is at the heart of the way you work.*

Further Reading

BACK K. *and* K. (1986) 'Assertiveness Training for Meetings' *Industrial and Commercial Training*, Vol. 18, No 2, March/April pp 26–30

BOYDELL T. *and* LEARY M. (1996) *Identifying Training Needs.* London, Chartered Institute of Personnel and Development

BRAMLEY P. (1996) *Evaluating Training.* London, Chartered Institute of Personnel and Development

CANNELL M. (2002) 'The Value of Learning' in *People Management.* 21 February 2002

FOWLER A. (1998) *Negotiating, Persuading and Influencing.* London, Chartered Institute of Personnel and Development

HACKETT P. (1996) *Success in Managing People.* London, John Murray

HARDINGHAM A. (1997) *Designing Training.* London, Chartered Institute of Personnel and Development

HARRISON R. (2002) *Learning and Development.* London. Chartered Institute of Personnel and Development

HOLLYFORDE S. *and* WHIDDETT S. (2002). *The Motivation Handbook.* London, Chartered Institute of Personnel and Development

HONEY P. *and* MUMFORD A. (1992) *The Manual of Learning Styles.* Maidenhead, Peter Honey

KOLB D. A. *et al* (1974) *Organisational Psychology: An Experiential Approach.* Hemel Hempstead, Prentice Hall

MARTIN M. *and* JACKSON T. (2000) *Personnel Practice.* London, Chartered Institute of Personnel and Development

MEGGINSON D. *and* WHITAKER V. (1996) *Cultivating Self-development.* London, Chartered Institute of Personnel and Development

MUMFORD A. (1997) *Management Development.* London, Chartered Institute of Personnel and Development

OTTO C. P. and GLASER R. O. (1970) *The Management of Training.* London, Addison Wesley

PEARNS M. *and* KANDOLA R. (1993) *Job Analysis: A practical guide for managers.* London, Institute of Personnel Management

REID M. A. *and* BARRINGTON H. (1999) *Training Interventions.* London, Chartered Institute of Personnel and Development

ROSSETT A. *The ASTD e-learning handbook: Best practice strategies and case studies for an emerging field.*

SIDDONS S. (1999) *Presentation Skills.* London, Chartered Institute of Personnel and Development

SLOMAN M. (2001) *The e-Learning Revolution.* London, Chartered Institute of Personnel and Development

WHITMORE J. (1992) *Coaching for Performance.* London, Nicholas Brealey

WILSON D. (2003) *Building the e-learning Organisation.* London, Chartered Institute of Personnel and Development

Index